W9-CEV-914

Basic
STAINED GLASS MAKING

All the Skills and Tools You Need to Get Started

Eric Ebeling, editor

Michael Johnston,
stained glass expert
and consultant

photographs by
Alan Wycheck

STACKPOLE
BOOKS

0 11557 02846 1

Copyright © 2003 by Stackpole Books

Published by
STACKPOLE BOOKS
5067 Ritter Road
Mechanicsburg, PA 17055
www.stackpolebooks.com

All rights reserved, including the right to reproduce this book or portions thereof in any form or by any means, electronic or mechanical, including photocopying, recording, or by any information storage and retrieval system, without permission in writing from the publisher. All inquiries should be addressed to Stackpole Books, 5067 Ritter Road, Mechanicsburg, Pennsylvania 17055.

Printed in the United States of America

20 19 18 17 16 15 14 13 12 11 10

First edition

Photographs by Alan Wycheck
Cover design by Tracy Patterson

Library of Congress Cataloging-in-Publication Data

Basic stained glass making : all the skills and tools you need to get started / Eric Ebeling, editor ; photographs by Alan Wycheck.— 1st ed.
    p. cm.
  ISBN 0-8117-2846-3
  1. Glass craft. 2. Glass painting and staining. I. Ebeling, Eric.
TT298 .B365 2003
748.5'028'2—dc21

                                        2003009605

ISBN 978-0-8117-2846-1

Contents

Acknowledgments

A number of people have helped to make this book possible, and I apologize to anyone I have failed to recognize properly here.

My gratitude to: Michael Johnston of Rainbow Visions Stained Glass in Harrisburg, Pa., whose teaching skills are surpassed only by his kindness and knowledge of stained glass making; Alan Wycheck of Wycheck Photography in Harrisburg, who uses his lens to see things the rest of us miss; Lee Summers, a stained glass craftsman whose yeoman's work made the photo shoots so much easier; Tracy Patterson and Wendy Reynolds, book designers, who managed to take so many little parts and turn them into one beautiful whole; Caroline Stover, art director, for her meticulous work with the art program for this book—a vast collection of images that left me cross-eyed more than once; Chris Chappell, for the admirable job keeping everything straight; and last, but far from least, my wife Andrea and son Alec, the world's finest support staff.

—Eric Ebeling

Introduction

This book contains all of the essential information and instruction that a beginner needs to know to make basic stained glass projects.

The material is presented in much the same way as a series of workshops on stained glass making. In fact, the hands-on approach here is based on the successful, time-tested classes taught at Rainbow Vision Stained Glass in Harrisburg, Pa., where thousands have become better at the craft.

As obvious as it sounds, you should begin reading from the front and continue through to the end without skipping around—each section in the book builds upon information contained in the previous one. You should familiarize yourself with workspace needs and stained glass safety before learning how to cut glass and solder. The projects themselves are arranged essentially by increasing difficulty, and the skills you learn in one section carry over in sequence to the next. The sample patterns printed at the back of the book can be used in any order once you have completed all of the detailed step-by-step projects.

Keep in mind that stained glass making, like any handcraft, takes time and patience to learn. Mistakes are inevitable, but they will become less common as you gain experience.

However, there is no such thing as perfection in stained glass making. Michael Johnston, owner of Rainbow Vision Stained Glass, likes to put it this way: "Great virtue can be made of slight irregularities."

1

A Good Work Environment

A beginner doesn't need to set up an elaborate workshop or studio to make the stained glass projects in this book—a simple clutter-free surface such as a workbench or table will work fine.

Glass cutting and other work should be done on top of a firm but cushioned surface, not a hard metal or wooden tabletop without any give. The gray-colored work surface shown here is a piece of Homasote fiberboard, manufactured by the Homasote Company of West Trenton, New Jersey. This board is made of recycled materials and is fire-resistant. It is a firm surface that has a slight spring to it. Tacks and nails can be driven into it easily, and a single section of it can last for years. Check your local hardware store or online for the availability of it or other material that can be used on the tabletop.

Consider establishing a work area in an empty corner of a low-traffic room, such as in the basement or garage, where sharp pieces of glass and chemicals won't pose a risk.

Keep in mind that each of the projects in this book involves lead-based solder or metal framing material, which should never be used in areas where food is stored. Certain chemicals that you will use are harmful if inhaled and should not be used in enclosed spaces, so make sure your work area has adequate ventilation.

Stained glass making also produces large quantities of glass shards that tend to get into every nook and cranny and are difficult to clean up completely. A handheld brush and dustpan can be used to sweep up glass chunks, as can a handheld vacuum. Many hobbyists have been surprised by the sharp sting of one of these hidden shards.

One specialized glass-cutting system developed by the Morton Company has a surface made up of recessed squares designed to catch and hold glass shards so they don't scatter. This system also uses trademarked measuring and gripping tools for cutting glass. Contact your local stained glass supplier or craft store for more information about the Morton glass-cutting system, or search for details online.

A handy supply of water—either from a faucet or from a container such as a large basin—is needed for each of the projects to wash away bits of glass, chemical residues, and the like. Keep a rag within easy reach for wiping oil off your hands while cutting glass.

Make sure an outlet for electricity is accessible near the work area to power the soldering iron and any other piece of equipment that requires it, such as an electric glass grinder or vacuum cleaner.

Sheets of stained glass should be stored vertically for easy access and safety. They can be carefully propped upright against a wall in an out-of-the-way location with an old blanket or piece of cardboard to cushion the bottom edges. You can also use old wooden crates or build a simple narrow rack with two sides and an open top to hold the sheets. Don't put the glass flat on the ground because it can be difficult to handle that way and may become damaged.

Quite a few tools are used to make stained glass projects, so you might find that a toolbox or small cabinet helps to keep them organized and easier to find when needed.

2

Stained Glass Safety

Keep these safety tips in mind when making stained glass projects.

- You must use care and common sense when working with cames and solder containing lead. As a general rule, stained glass hobbyists are exposed to very low levels of lead while making their projects. However, any time lead is present in the environment, it should be handled and used responsibly. Prolonged exposure to high levels of lead can pose significant health risks: It has been linked to brain and nerve damage in children, and it can cause such problems as high blood pressure, nerve disorders, and memory and concentration problems in adults, according to information from the United States Environmental Protection Agency.
- Pregnant or nursing women should avoid contact with all stained glass materials containing lead.
- Never eat, drink, or smoke when working with lead.
- It is a good idea to wear the same work clothes each time you make stained glass. Keep these clothes in your work area, because lead dust can collect in your clothing and can be carried throughout your living space.
- Wear enclosed shoes, such as boots that lace up, to prevent dust from collecting on your feet.
- Children must be supervised at all times when working with stained glass materials.
- Do not allow pets into the work area.
- Always wear rubber gloves when working with patinas and etching creams. These substances can cause chemical burns on exposed skin and can be harmful if absorbed into the blood stream.
- Keep a supply of adhesive bandages handy for the small nicks and cuts that are virtually unavoidable when working with glass. A first aid kit containing antiseptic, some gauze pads, a few larger butterfly-style bandages for somewhat deeper wounds, and similar supplies is a good idea to have within easy reach.
- Stained glass making requires your full attention. You should avoid working on projects when you are fatigued or distracted; instead, wait for a more appropriate time.
- Frequently brush away glass shards from your work surface and into a dustpan. This will help to reduce the risk of receiving cuts to your hands or forearms when leaning on the table. NEVER try to wipe away glass bits or dust with your bare hand!
- Use care when handling large sheets of glass. You should carefully grip the sheet by the top edge and hold it perpendicular to the floor, moving it slowly and carefully to avoid jarring it. Never hold a large piece of glass horizontally because it might crack from the strain, and never hold glass above your head. Never try to catch a piece of falling glass; it's best to let it go and try to move quickly out of the way.
- Always wear safety glasses or goggles when cutting and polishing glass, even if the task takes only a few seconds.
- To avoid burns, place a hot soldering iron in an appropriate stand away from the work area when not in use. Do not put the soldering iron down on the work surface, where it might roll or be bumped accidentally. Do not inhale the fumes produced by hot flux and solder, and read the labels on these products for additional information regarding safety issues.

3

Equipment and Materials

Take some time to learn about the materials and equipment needed for successful stained glass making. Some of the items listed on the following pages might be in your toolbox or workshop right now. Other more specialized pieces of equipment need to be purchased at a craft or hardware store, stained glass shop, or from an online source.

Each project in this book requires a different combination of the equipment and materials explained in this section. A checklist is included at the start of each project specifying all the tools and materials you will need to complete it. This list can be copied and taken along to the store with you when you go shopping.

GLASS CUTTERS

A quality glass cutter is among the most important tools a beginner must have before starting a project. All cutters consist of a handle and a metal wheel of some type that turns against the glass to create a weakened seam called a score.

This wheel, which rotates much like a pizza cutter, is not at all sharp. It must be lubricated before each cut to reduce friction between the blade and the glass.

Less expensive cutters usually require manual lubrication, whereas the more expensive ones are designed to be self-lubricating.

Each type of cutter listed will work well for the stained glass projects in this book. Keep in mind that learning to use a cutter correctly takes some patience and some practice, as the exercises on page 24–42 will demonstrate.

CARBIDE STEEL WHEEL CUTTER

The most inexpensive and "low-tech" of all cutters, this type uses a rotating wheel of honed steel to score and weaken the surface of the glass before breaking. The wheel must be manually lubricated before every cut to reduce friction on the glass that might shatter or chip it. The steel cutting wheel can be replaced when it becomes dull. The grip typically is made of metal, plastic, or wood and is designed to fit well in the hand. Most have a weighty ball on the back end of the grip for tapping scored glass, and three indentations near the tip that can break or chip glass if needed. Approximate cost: $15.

TUNGSTEN CARBIDE WHEEL CUTTER

This type uses tungsten, a very hard metallic element, in the cutting wheel. This makes it more durable than the steel type and allows it to cut much more efficiently and with much less force.

The plastic handle of the cutter serves as a reservoir for the oil that needs to be applied to the wheel before cutting; lubricant is added through a small hole in the handle. The grip is designed to fit well in the hand, and the ball at the back end of the grip can be used to tap and separate cut pieces of glass. Approximate cost: $30.

PISTOL GRIP WHEEL CUTTER

This variation on the standard tungsten carbide wheel cutter replaces the simple shaft with a pistol grip for easier and more precise handling. The handle is hollow and holds the glass cutting oil.

The liquid flows from the reservoir down to the wheel through a small tip that contains an absorbent wick. A spring mechanism squeezes out lubrication every time downward force is applied to the cutter.

Many stained glass hobbyists prefer this kind of cutter because it helps to reduce some of the hand fatigue that might occur with a standard cutter, and it allows greater control over cutting in some instances. Approximate cost: $35.

CUTTING OIL

A number of manufacturers sell oil specially designed for use with glass cutters. The oil helps to reduce friction between the wheel and glass surface, and it also helps to keep small flecks of glass from impeding the rotation of the wheel. As a household substitute, kerosene may also be used as a lubricant. Approximate cost: $5 per bottle.

4

SOLDERING IRON

The soldering iron is used to melt lead solder, which is used to join two or more pieces of metal together. You should select an iron rated between 75 and 200 watts. A number of models come equipped with an adjustable control on them for maintaining a specific temperature; other models can be plugged into a separate rheostat unit and adjusted that way. A different kind of iron uses interchangeable tips to regulate temperature.

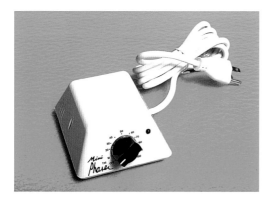

A sturdy stand is recommended for convenience and safety. The stand usually consists of a heavy, stable base with a coiled piece of metal attached for holding the iron when it's not in use. This helps to prevent accidental burns and keeps the iron from being dropped or knocked to the floor.

Most stands typically have a small tray in the base where a moist sponge is placed for periodically wiping solder and flux residue off the hot iron. Approximate cost: $10–$40, depending on the model; the stand will cost under $10.

SOLDER

The solder used in stained glass making is an alloy—or mixture—of tin and lead that is melted with a hot soldering iron and applied to pieces of metal or foil to bond them together. The most common solders are sold in wrapped spools and are available with either a 50–50 ratio of tin to lead or a 60–40 ratio of tin to lead. The latter solder is more expensive because of its composition, but it flows smoothly and is generally easier to work with than the 50–50 blend. Approximate cost: $5 per 1-pound spool.

FLUX

Used to clean oxidation and other dirt from metal surfaces so that melted solder will adhere readily. Without flux, solder would simply not stick to the foiled edges of glass or to lead supports. Flux can be found in liquid, gel, or paste form, and each works well for foil and lead projects. Because it is corrosive, care must be taken when using it. Some manufacturers sell types of flux designed to emit less smoke and fumes than other brands. Check labeling. Approximate cost: $5–$15.

FLUX BRUSH

Any medium-to-firm brush designed to apply paint or solvent-type materials can be used. Approximate cost: $1.

CUTTING SQUARE

Used much like a ruler, the cutting square is designed to gauge straight lines based on a right angle, which is helpful when drawing shapes such as squares and rectangles. A raised lip along the underside of one edge of the square keeps it from moving when you're cutting a right angle. Approximate cost: $10.

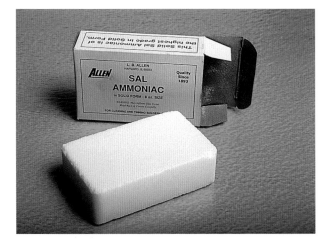

RULER

Used as a measuring tool and to make straight, even lines while drawing or cutting. A ruler backed with cork or other skid-resistant material is a good choice. Approximate cost: $5.

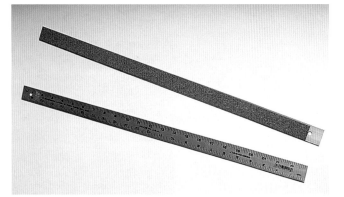

SOLDER IRON TIP CLEANER (SAL AMMONIAC)

Sal ammoniac is a naturally occurring or man-made mineral composed of ammonium chloride that reacts to the heat of a soldering iron and helps to clean residue from it when the iron is gently scraped across it. Approximate cost: $5.

PATTERN SHEARS

These special scissors are designed so one blade fits inside the other, delivering a cut that removes a thin strip of paper between the two pieces being cut. This strip is important for stained glass making because it indicates the gap that must be left between pieces of the project when it is being built. Typically, shears are available that leave a gap of $^1/_{32}$ of an inch for foil-edged projects and a gap of $^1/_{16}$ of an inch for lead projects.

Some manufacturers produce a model of scissors with an interchangeable blade that can handle both kinds of cutting widths.

It also is a good idea to keep a regular pair of scissors nearby for routine cutting and trimming. Approximate cost: $10–$20.

GROZING PLIERS

Used to remove uneven or jagged pieces of glass left after cutting. These pliers have relatively narrow, serrated jaws for gripping even small chunks of glass.

One side of the jaws typically is curved and the other straight; the tips of the jaws close perfectly flush to each other, which is necessary when they are used to "chew" and grind away glass. This tool also can be used to snap glass along a scored line. Also called grozing-breaking pliers. Approximate cost: $8–$30.

RUNNING PLIERS

These thick pliers are used to carefully break a piece of glass along a score line made by a cutter. One top jaw of the pliers is flat, while the bottom contains a narrow, raised section in the center of it. This raised section is positioned under the score line; when the pliers are squeezed firmly together, the force causes the glass to break evenly along the score. These are especially helpful when cutting long strips of glass. Approximate cost: $8.

NEEDLE-NOSE STYLE PLIERS
Good to have for small detail work on a number of projects.

WIRE CUTTERS
Used to cut pieces of reinforcing wire and picture hanging wire.

HAMMER OR MALLET
A mallet with one head made of rubber is a good choice for stained glass making; sometimes glass pieces need to be tapped gently into place, and the rubber reduces the risk of cracking.

CARBORUNDUM STONE
A trademarked name for a coarse, abrasive tool used to smooth jagged edges of glass. Water should be applied to the stone periodically to reduce friction between it and the glass, which will make smoothing easier. Approximate cost: $6.

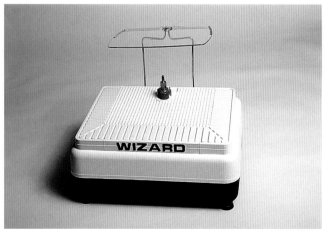

ELECTRIC GLASS GRINDER
These commercial grinders take the place of a grinding stone and instead use a spinning wheel to shave off sharp edges of glass until they are smooth. They are designed to be used on the tabletop, and most feature an eye protection guard and a small, water-filled chamber that keeps the grinding wheel lubricated during operation. Approximate cost: $80–$250, depending on model.

8

COPPER FOIL

This ribbonlike shiny foil is applied carefully to the edge of a cut piece of glass and wrapped so that it covers a portion of both sides of the glass. It provides a surface to which solder can bond. Most foil sold for stained glass making comes in tapelike rolls and is backed with adhesive for easy application. Standard widths are $3/16$ inch, $7/32$ inch, and $1/4$ inch; the aesthetic nature of the project will help determine whether the foil used should be subtle and dainty (thin) or robust and strong (thick). A foil with a black-colored backing also is available for use in projects where a copper look is not desired. Approximate cost for a 36-yard roll: $10.

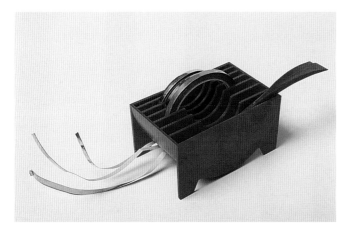

COPPER FOIL DISPENSER

Several manufacturers sell dispensers designed to make foiling easier and more efficient. Most operate like dispensers for adhesive tape with either a vertical or horizontal orientation; features range from the basic to the elaborate. Foiling by hand is recommended for beginners until the technique is understood well. Approximate cost: $10–$50, depending on model.

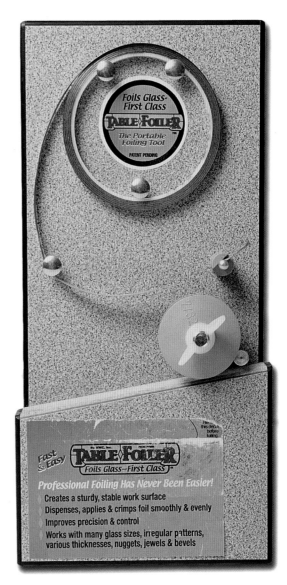

Equipment and Materials

LEAD CAMES

These are long strips of pliable lead, usually sold in sections 4 to 6 feet long, that make up the entire framework for leaded glass projects. They have a central channel that holds pieces of glass in place, provides the metal surface needed for soldering, and establishes the lines and curves that define a project.

As shown in Figures 1 and 2, most cames have channels that are either H-shaped (left) for holding two pieces of glass along a shared edge or U-shaped (right) for holding a single piece along an outside edge.

Pieces of brass or copper (Figure 3, left and right) are available for projects that require a golden or coppery appearance. Zinc channel (Figure 3, center), a very sturdy and rigid material, can be used as well. Approximate cost: $3 per 6-foot-long strip of lead; prices of the other materials are somewhat higher.

Note: Please read the section on stained glass safety for information about the safe handling, use, and storage of lead materials.

LEAD VISE

This simple metal vise is used to hold a strip of lead came in place so that it can be stretched before use. This stretching makes the came firmer and easier to use. Approximate cost: $5.

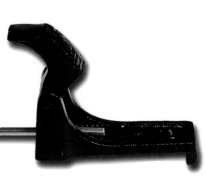

LEAD CUTTERS

These snips, also called lead pliers, have blades that are flat on one side and concave on the other to cut lead cames sharply at an angle. Use a pair of these when cutting cames for use as corner pieces. Approximate cost: $10–$30.

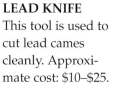

LEAD KNIFE

This tool is used to cut lead cames cleanly. Approximate cost: $10–$25.

HORSESHOE NAILS

These long, narrow nails are flat on one side, making them perfect for holding a wooden frame or jig in place during project building. They are usually sold in packs of one or two dozen. Approximate cost: $5 per pack.

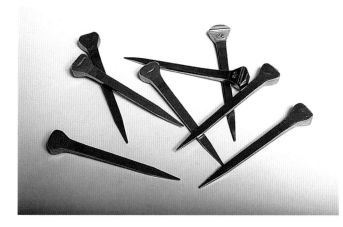

DUSTPAN AND BRUSH

A standard brush and dustpan are perfect for sweeping up shards of glass from the work area to eliminate the risk of injury.

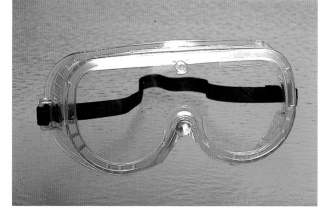

SAFETY GOGGLES

These should be worn for eye protection while breaking or grinding glass.

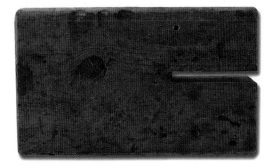

WOODEN BLOCK HOLDER
A basic wooden block with a notch cut in the center can be used to hold a sheet of glass.

MASKING TAPE
Has a variety of uses, such as holding paper patterns in place.

PICTURE HANGING WIRE
Attach this to the back of mirrors and other projects that need to be hung.

LEAD BOARD WITH RIGHT ANGLE
This board is used to hold the side and bottom of a lead project in place while it is being put together. A lead board can be made easily by nailing two furring strips of equal size—18 inches will work for many small and moderate size projects—at a right angle to each other.

WOODEN OR PLASTIC FID

This tool comes in a number of shapes and sizes and is used mainly as a burnishing or smoothing tool when applying foil to stained glass. It also can be used to gently pry open the channel portion of a piece of lead came. Approximate cost: $1–$2.

GLAZING CEMENT

This is spread in a thick coat across a leaded stained glass project to seal and strengthen the joint areas formed by lead cames. The putty, which typically comes packed in linseed oil, must be mixed well before use. Approximate cost: $10 per 1-pound tub.

WHITING

Whiting is a white powder, typically composed of calcium carbonate, that is used to dry the glazing cement and allow it to set. Whiting also helps to clean excess putty from the glass surface. Approximate cost: $2.50 per 1-pound bag.

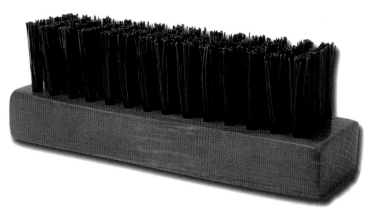

BRUSH

Used for applying lead cement. Choose a stiff-bristle brush about 6 inches wide, like the kind used for scrubbing floors. Approximate cost: $5.

PATINA

A patina is a liquid solution that is applied to solder with a cloth or brush to change its appearance. The liquid changes solder from silver to a dark gray or black color; certain kinds are formulated to make the solder appear to have a copper tone. Patina contains chemicals that are harmful to the skin and lungs, so it must be used with care and caution.

A stained glass piece should be rinsed with warm soapy water after the patina is applied to neutralize the chemical reaction and make it safe to handle.

Fire grate blackener is a similar substance used to darken lead cames at the end of a project. Approximate cost: $5.

RUBBER GLOVES

Must be used when working with patina.

FLUX REMOVER

Available in many craft stores, this substance neutralizes chemicals in flux and patina, and will need to be applied at the end of several projects. Approximate cost: $10.

MIRROR SEALER

This aerosol spray is used to cover the backside of a mirror to keep the reflective coating from getting damaged. Approximate cost: $10.

FINISHING COMPOUND

Applied as the last step to a project, this waxlike compound helps to polish the piece so that it shines while coating it to retard oxidation and tarnish buildup. Approximate cost: $10.

WIRE AND OTHER FASTENERS

You can choose from a variety of wires, chains, and rings in designing stained glass hangings.

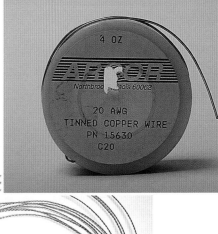

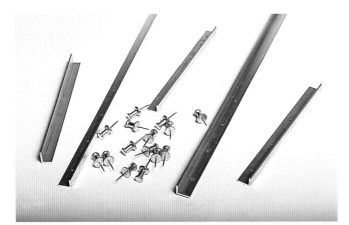

PUSHPINS, TACKS, AND JIG MATERIAL

These items are needed at certain times to hold projects in place while you are working on them.

CRAFT KNIFE

This is the perfect tool for repairing small mistakes in copper foil and for other small tasks.

STEEL WOOL

Used to remove oxidized material from solder and other metal parts.

PLASTIC BASIN AND SPONGE

Holds warm soapy water so the projects can be cleaned of glass shards and other debris.

CLOTH RAG

Good to keep handy.

CARBON PAPER
This is the inky blue or black paper used to transfer the pattern of the project onto heavy stock paper.

OAK TAG
This paper has a thickness and texture similar to a manila file folder or thin piece of cardboard. It is used to make patterns.

TRACING PAPER
This very thin paper is translucent and allows the lines from the original pattern to show through so they can be traced.

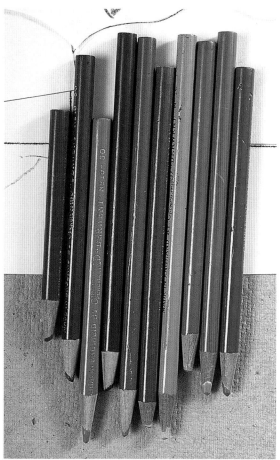

RUBBER CEMENT
Used to glue paper templates onto pieces of glass prior to cutting.

COLORED PENCILS
These are used on a paper pattern to indicate a corresponding stained glass color, which helps to eliminate confusion after the pattern is cut.

Keep a supply of standard pencils, pens, and markers on hand for drawing patterns, marking measurements, and the like.

4

Understanding Glass

Generally speaking, most stained glass is created when a mixture of sand, ash, metal oxide colorings, and other ingredients is heated to incredibly high temperatures until it becomes a molten liquid. This liquid is then either blown or rolled and allowed to cool into solid sheets of glass. This process can occur either by hand or with the help of machinery; each technique can significantly alter the appearance, texture, and price of the glass.

Experts place all glass into one of two categories: cathedral and opalescent.

Cathedral glass is transparent or very translucent, meaning that light can pass through it easily; these characteristics are perfect for most types of stained glass projects, such as those designed to be backlit by the sun or by an incandescent source. Cathedrals are made in many colors and textures, and most are great for use by beginners because they are fairly easy to cut.

Some typical examples are smooth cathedral, hammered cathedral, and granite cathedral.

Smooth cathedral

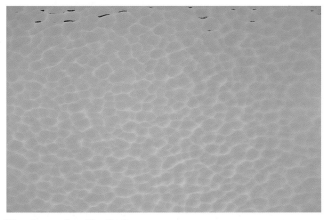

Hammered cathedral

Granite cathedral

Opalescents, also referred to as opals, don't transmit as much light as cathedrals because the glass has a milky, dense quality to it. Most opals are considered to be semitranslucent, meaning they allow some—but not all—light to pass through it. Some opals are virtually opaque and allow no light to penetrate at all.

Some typical examples are multicolor opal and solid opal.

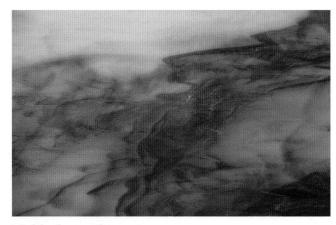

Multicolor opal

Solid opal

Within the cathedral and opalescent categories of glass exists a nearly limitless variety of colors, textures, patterns, and properties:

Seedy glass gives the appearance of tiny grains suspended in the glass.

Shown here with a black background for contrast.

Reamy Baroque features swirls and whorls.

Glue chip glass has a frostlike appearance.

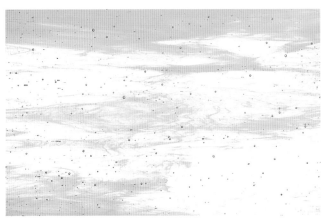

Water glass has a wet, flowing look to it.

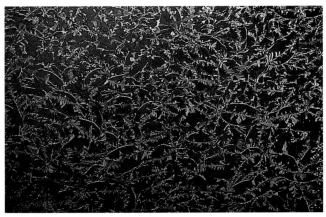

Shown here with a black background for contrast.

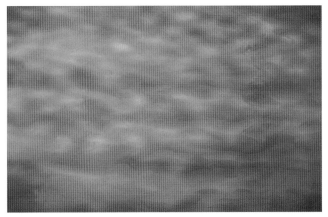

Streaky glass contains veins of contrasting color.

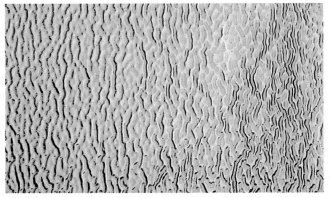

Ripple glass has a raised texture.

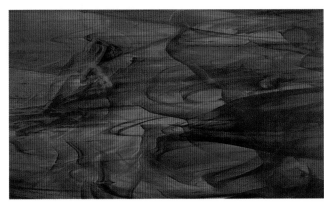

Wispy glass has the quality of drifting sand.

19

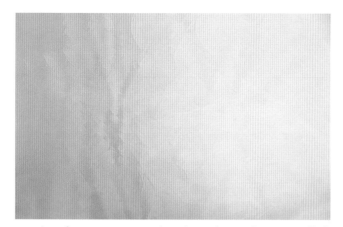

Another common variety is **antique glass,** so called not because of its age but because of the traditional way it is produced: the glass is heated and blown into thin sheets that are then allowed to cool. Antique glass can be a little more expensive than other kinds of glass because it is more labor-intensive to create.

Iridescent glass is a shimmering type that is created through the use of metallic elements that are fused with the glass.

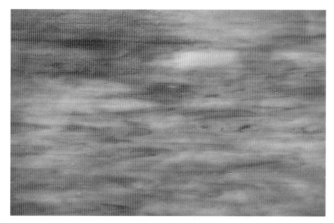

Iridescent opal

Iridescent clear Krinkle

Another general subcategory of glass is **art glass.** Much of this glass is produced and trademarked by specific manufacturers. It can have characteristics of cathedrals and opals, and it generally is high-quality and a bit more expensive than mass-produced glass.

Here are some examples:

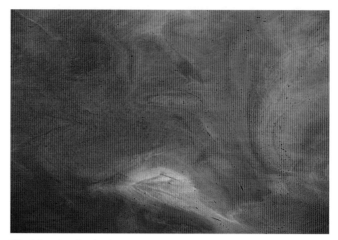

Multicathedral glass

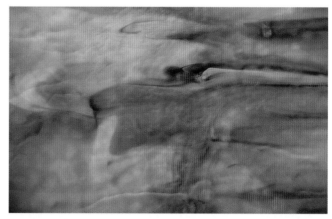

Mottled glass

Granite back glass

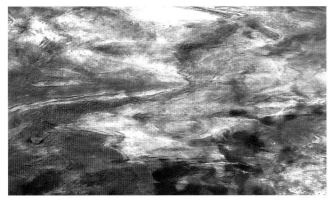

Stipple glass

Fracture and streamer glass

You also should be familiar with unique kinds of glass such as bevels, nuggets, and jewels.

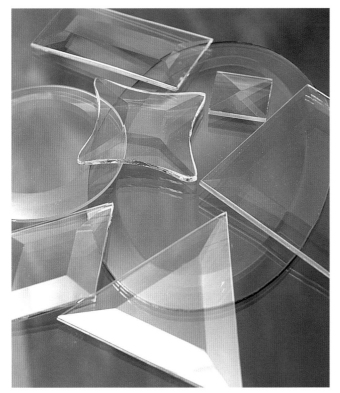

Bevels are pre-cut chunks of glass with angled edges that help refract light somewhat like a prism. They are generally clear, and cannot be cut easily.

Nuggets are smooth, rounded, somewhat flat "drops" of cool glass that are used to adorn a variety of projects.

Jewels are hunks of glass that have been manufactured to simulate jewels or precious stones. These have a number of applications, and they come in many shapes and sizes.

Finally, you can find **mirrored glass** on any household mirror. It is simply a transparent glass backed by a shiny silver surface that reflects light.

Because of the large number of choices available, buying glass can be a bit tricky at first. While there are no real "wrong" selections, you may want to ask for help from your stained glass shop or glass supplier to find some that are easy to cut and that have the properties you need for your project. Otherwise, just pick the glass that has the color and appearance you find to be aesthetically pleasing. If you have difficulty finding the kinds of glass you want at a local stained glass shop, there are many stained glass outlets on the Internet.

5

Basic Skills

Glass Cutting

No other part of stained glass making strikes as much fear in the hearts of beginners as glass cutting. Most approach a sheet of stained glass timidly at first, afraid of shattering it or—worse yet—being injured by it. You will find out quickly that stained glass is surprisingly strong and might even resist some strong attempts to crack it; and you will also learn that, with the exception of a small nick or two, stained glass is safe if you use common sense while working with it.

A point of clarification: The term "glass cutting" is a bit misleading. You actually use a glass cutter (see pages 3–4 for additional information about cutters) to score a piece of glass—like putting a deep scratch into it—before snapping the piece along the score line. Glass is typically made up of tiny pieces of sandlike grains of silica that have been fused together under high heat and allowed to cool; the carbide wheel of your glass cutter separates these microscopic particles as it scratches a groove in the glass. This groove represents a line of weakness where the glass can be snapped cleanly by placing pressure on either side of it, a technique that is explained a bit later.

Scoring and breaking glass cleanly and accurately are very important to the overall quality of the finished piece, as are the techniques of grozing and grinding glass, explained later on.

Holding the Cutter

Many beginners find the pistol-grip cutter to be the easiest to handle and control because it is designed to fit comfortably in your hand, but with practice, you will become proficient using any kind of cutter.

Grip the cutter naturally in your dominant hand—the one you write with—and place your thumb in a comfortable position along the top edge; your palm will help regulate the amount of downward pressure you put on the glass while scoring it. Make sure the position of the cutter feels comfortable in your hand, because muscle cramping and hand fatigue can set in quickly with an unnatural grip.

It is recommended that you use your other hand for added control when using the cutter. A good way to do this is to cup this hand against the other one while overlapping your thumbs, as shown. Place the index finger of the less-dominant hand along the edge of the shaft holding the cutting wheel. This finger will help to give you greater

control of the cutter and keep it moving straight across the glass.

If you are using the traditional wheel cutter, slide it between the first two fingers of your dominant hand and close your index finger and thumb down on the cutter.

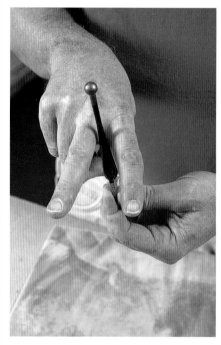

Your index finger will act as a guide to keep the cutter moving straight.

Place the thumb of your other hand on the top of the cutter; this will help provide downward pressure while cutting. Now place the index finger of that hand onto the edge of the shaft holding the cutting wheel; this will help guide the cutter. You also can hold this cutter the way you would a pencil, or grip it in your fist the way a child draws with a crayon.

Keep in mind that the instructions given here for holding a glass cutter are just suggestions; the way in which you hold your cutter is largely a matter of preference, and you should try a variety of grips until you find the one that suits you best.

Cutting the Glass

Put on your safety goggles.

Place a small scrap piece of glass on your work table, preferably on top of a piece of Homasote fiberboard (see page 1) or other material that will cushion it and help hold it in place. Make sure the cutting wheel is lubricated, or the score will likely be a bad one. If the cutter is not a self-lubricating model, you should dip the cutting wheel in lubricant after each cut. One easy way to do this is to tap it against a sponge or rag soaked in oil. Even the wheel of a self-lubricating model should be checked periodically for a buildup of glass powder.

Put the wheel down on the side of the glass nearest you, as close to the front edge as possible. For this practice cut, make sure there will be at least an inch of glass on either side of the score when you are done to make breaking easier. Apply firm downward pressure—not with full strength, but with enough force for the wheel to make contact with the glass without slipping.

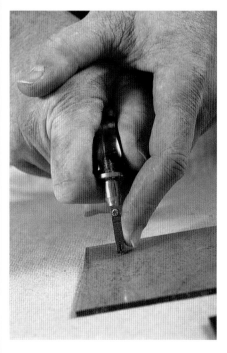

Pressing down too hard may cause the glass to crack; if your line ends up looking white and powdery, you probably are pushing down too hard. Pressing down too lightly may allow the wheel to slip or may produce an incomplete cut.

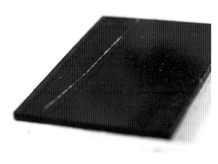

While applying this pressure, slowly push the cutter forward so the carbide wheel turns against the glass. Move the tool at a steady, even pace to help make the score line consistent. A good score sounds gritty as it is being made—much like a piece of paper being torn in half.

Make sure the cutter is perpendicular to the glass and not leaning to the right or left at all, or the glass might not be scored properly. Similarly, make sure the cutter remains level, not tilted too far forward or backward; this also helps you to keep an unobstructed visual path to the template you are cutting. Some experts prefer to make cuts by dragging the tool back toward them, but this technique is trickier to learn and is not recommended for a beginner.

Stop your cut as close to the far edge of the glass as you can without actually touching it, around $1/8$ inch away.

Cutting all the way to the edge can cause the glass to crack and splinter, which could ruin the piece you are scoring.

Take Note

Never go back and try to score over a cut you have already made. The glass could break unpredictably, and you run the risk of damaging the cutting wheel. Just make a completely new cut.

Follow the same tips detailed previously when using a traditional cutter.

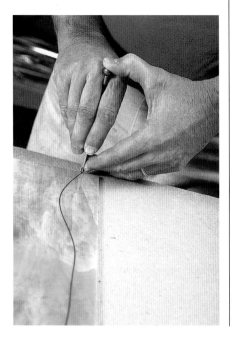

It is now time to break the glass along the score you just made. Make sure your hands are dry and free of lubricant.

Grip the piece of glass so that your thumbs rest on either side of the score, which is marked here with a white dot for illustrative purposes.

Your two index fingers should securely grip the underside of the glass on either side of the score.

Hold the piece firmly and, with a quick, snapping wrist motion, rotate both hands out and away from each other. If you scored the glass correctly, it will break cleanly along that line.

Never try to break the glass using an inward motion! This puts pressure on the strong and unscored underside of the glass first and could instantly shatter the glass in your hands.

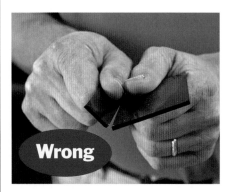

Wrong

Sometimes you will make a score that is difficult to break with your hands, particularly when there isn't enough glass on either side of the score to get a firm grip. The perfect tool in this situation is a pair of breaking pliers, which are commonly manufactured to do double duty as both breaking and grozing pliers, which saves on the cost of having to buy two different kinds.

You must pay special attention to the way in which this tool is used: In one direction, the tool uses a flat jaw designed for breaking only; in the other, it uses a curved jaw designed only for grozing or biting off bits of glass.

For use in breaking, the flattened top jaw of the pliers must be placed on the top surface of the glass that bears the score line. Notice how the pliers remain level while gripping the glass.

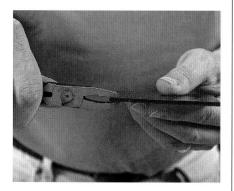

When used the other way around, the pliers do not grip the glass evenly, as shown.

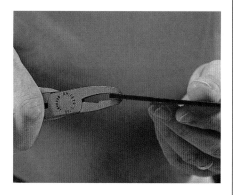

Place a marking, such as a line from an indelible pen, to indicate the flattened top jaw; it will save you time and help to avoid confusion when you are in the middle of a project.

Another useful tool for breaking glass is a pair of running pliers, so named because they cause the glass to crack or "run" cleanly along a score line. These wide-jawed pliers typically come with a white line on them to designate the top jaw . . .

. . . and a bottom jaw that features a raised lip in its center.

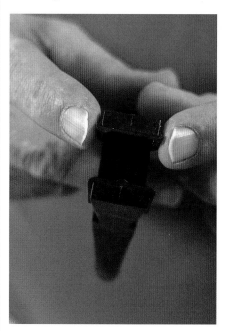

The pliers are placed at the edge of a piece of glass with the raised lip positioned under the score line to act as a fulcrum or pressure point. Squeezing the pliers together forces the glass to gently separate along the score.

At times you will find yourself cutting and separating long, thin strips of glass.

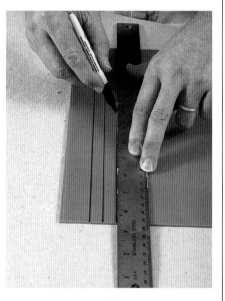

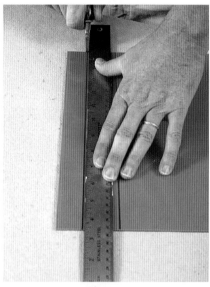

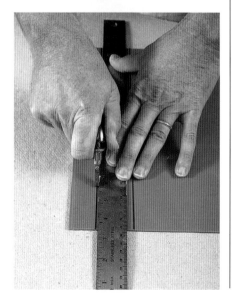

Running pliers are helpful in these situations. The design of the pliers allows the score in the glass to run uniformly as it breaks, greatly reducing the chances that the piece will snap. This holds true for straight cuts and curved scores as well.

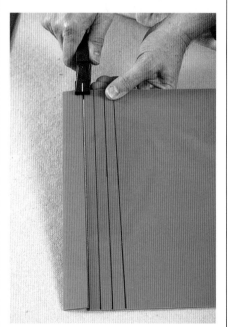

Practice scoring glass and breaking the pieces using the different tools until you feel comfortable with each.

There are two methods commonly used to score glass: freehand scoring and template scoring. With freehand scoring, a pattern is placed under a piece of glass and a cutter is used to carefully cut out the shapes as they show through. This method is not for beginners and takes a lot of practice to master.

Template scoring is a much more common method in which pieces of a paper pattern—called templates—are glued to the glass and then cut out. A number of sample templates appear on the pages that follow. Think of them as guides used to eliminate the guesswork from cutting.

Cutting Different Shapes

Every piece of stained glass you ever cut will consist of straight lines, concave curves (those that bend toward the inside of the piece), convex curves (those that bend away), or a combination of all three. The following exercises will lead you through the fundamentals of making these kinds of cuts, skills that will prepare you to tackle all of the stained glass projects in this book.

It is strongly suggested that you score and break the glass in these three essential shapes as many times as it takes until you feel prepared to cut them for an actual project. While you must concentrate on cutting the three shapes explained here in detail, a number of shape variations are provided on pages 40–42 for additional practice if you feel the need.

Shape A

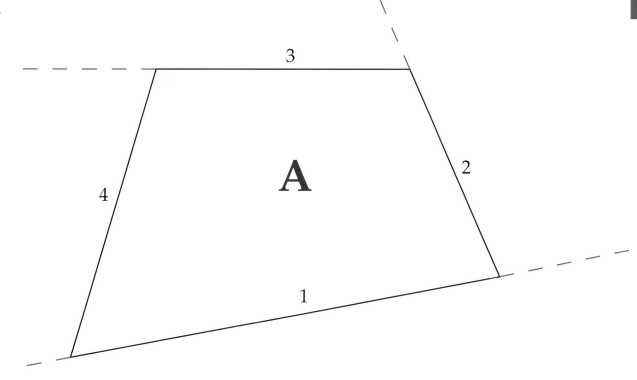

Note: The numbers indicate the recommended order in which you make your cuts.

Start with a piece of scrap glass that measures roughly 5 inches by 4 inches.

Redraw Shape A onto a piece of paper or photocopy it to make a template, then cut it out with scissors and use rubber cement to glue it directly onto the glass.

(For clarity in illustrating the cutting technique at this point, we have simply drawn the shape onto the glass with a white marking pen; you should use a paper template when you practice these cuts.)

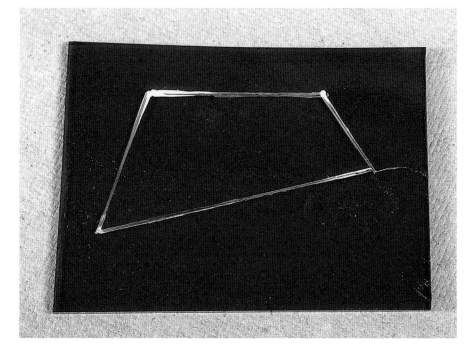

Remember to hold the cutter comfortably and keep the piece at a comfortable distance from your body so you don't have to stretch to reach it. Begin cutting one of the sides, using the outside edge of the line or template as your guide. On this piece, the order in which you make your cuts is not critical because all of the sides are basically the same. When making more complicated cuts, you should study the template and try to visualize how each score will affect subsequent scores.

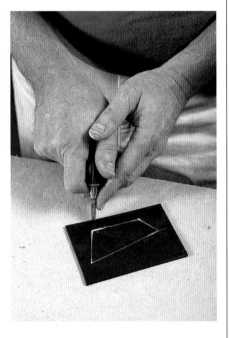

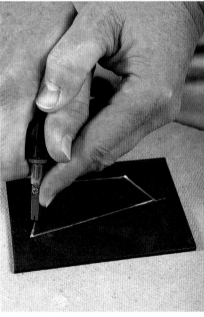

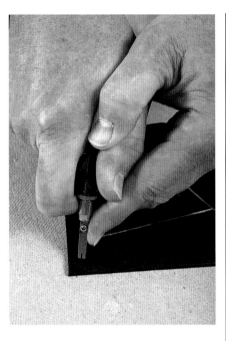

Break the glass along the score you just made. Remember to use breaking pliers if you can't get a good grip on any piece of glass you are trying to break.

Score and break another side of the shape.

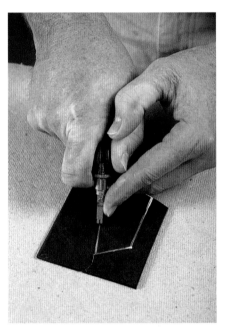

Do the same for the third side.

Score the last side.

Because the glass alongside the score was too narrow to grip by hand, breaking pliers were needed here to separate the pieces.

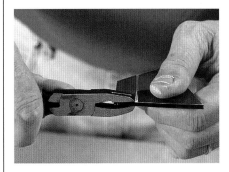

Don't worry if the edges of the piece are rough; this is normal. Techniques for grozing and grinding the edges—used to smooth the glass—will be explained later in this chapter. Just set the shape you cut aside until it is needed again.

It's time to move on to the next practice shape.

Shape B

This shape combines the straight-line cutting you have learned with an inside curve, which can be tricky to score.

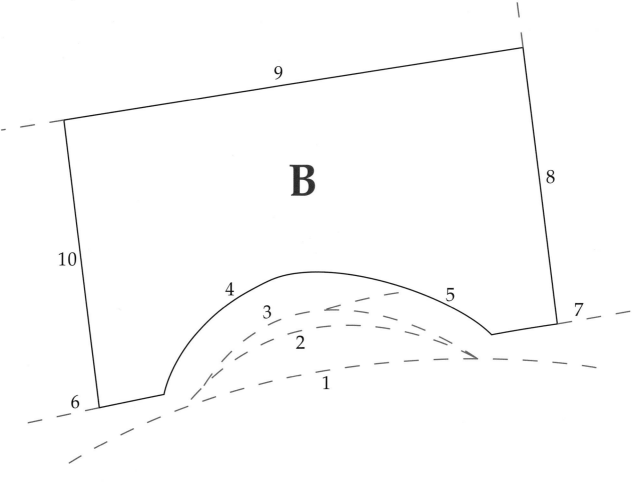

Start with a piece of scrap glass that measures roughly 6 inches by 6 inches.

Redraw Shape B onto a piece of paper or photocopy it to make a template, then cut it out with scissors, and use rubber cement to glue it directly onto the glass.

(For clarity in illustrating the cutting technique at this point, we have simply drawn the shape onto the glass with a black marker; you should use a paper template when you practice these cuts.)

An inside curve like this one must be carved out through a series of small, archlike cuts that remove sections of glass gradually to reduce the risk of accidental cracking. The paths of these arcs are indicated here with black marker. If you simply ran the cutter along the inside curve in one score and tried to break it, the properties of the glass would most likely cause the piece to split jaggedly outward toward the edges. It is always best to cut away small sections of glass instead of large hunks whenever possible.

Use your cutter to score the glass in an arc, as indicated by the bottom-most line shown here.

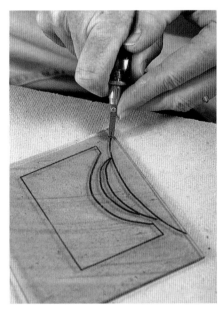

Gently snap this chunk away and discard it. You most likely will need to use pliers to do this.

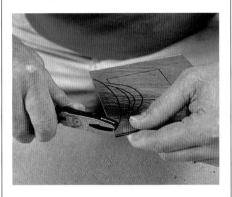

Score the next arc.

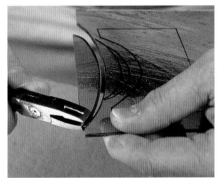

Gently break out this chunk.

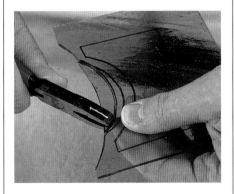

Score the next arc.

Gently break out this chunk.

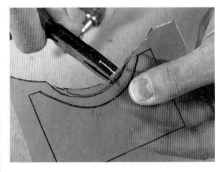

Now that much of the excess glass surrounding the inside curve has been removed, even smaller amounts of glass must be taken away to maintain the strength of the curve. As the marking pen indicates, the next cut will hug the inside edge of the curve to about a third of the way into the arc, where it will continue to the edge of the glass.

Score the glass as shown.

Remove this piece of glass.

Repeat the same type of cut on the other part of the inside curve.

Remove this piece of glass.

Now score the glass along the outside edge of the curve.

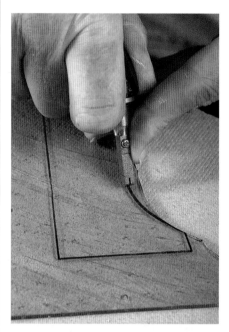

Remove this piece of glass.

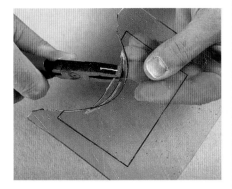

Don't worry if the curve you just cut isn't completely even or smooth at this point. You will learn how to smooth the edges a bit later.

Now is a good time to use a brush and a dustpan to clean glass shards off the work area.

To finish cutting this practice piece, trim the point of excess glass protruding from one of the sides.

Break it off.

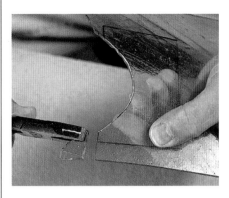

Now score the glass along the outside edge on the same side.

Make sure to continue the score as far as possible to the edge.

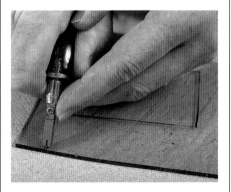

Break the glass at the score. Use running pliers if necessary to separate the pieces.

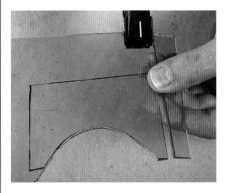

Now score a line across the excess glass on the other side of the curve.

Break it off.

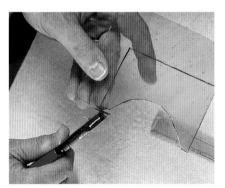

Score the outside edge.

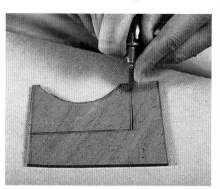

Break the glass.

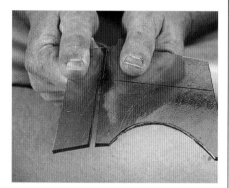

Score the last edge of the piece.

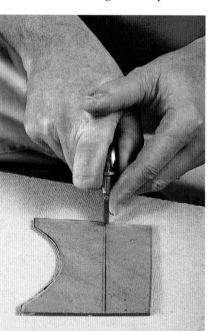

Break it off. A score like this breaks well with running pliers.

Congratulations. You've successfully cut the second practice pattern. Set it aside for now; you will smooth the edges of it a bit later.

Shape C

This circle shape contains a convex arc that is the opposite of the inside curve you just finished cutting.

2

C

1

3

4

Start with a piece of scrap glass that measures roughly 6 inches by 6 inches.

Redraw Shape C onto a piece of paper (the inside edge of a roll of masking tape works well for tracing) or photocopy it to make a template, then cut it out with scissors and use rubber cement to glue it directly onto the glass.

(As with the previous two cutting exercises, we have simply drawn the shape onto the glass with a black marker for clarity in illustrating the cutting technique; you should use a paper template when you practice these cuts to gain familiarity with the technique.)

You must cut this shape as a series of arcs with gentle curves, as indicated by the black pen lines.

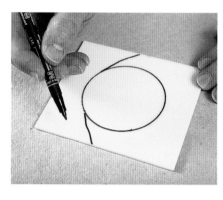

Begin cutting at the edge nearest you and continue in one fluid motion until you reach the other edge.

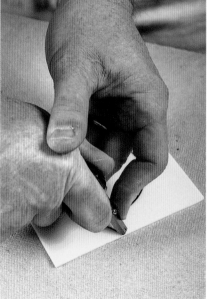

Break the glass along the score line you just made.

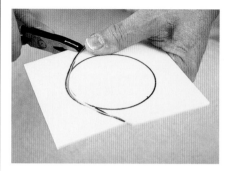

The next score you make will be just like the previous one—a gentle extension of the circle's curved edge.

Score the glass, using a fluid motion, until your cutting wheel reaches the far edge.

38

Break the glass along the score.

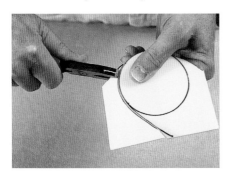

The next cut you make will be similar to the previous ones.

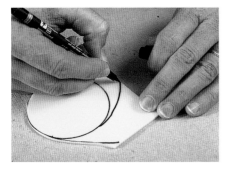

Score the glass along this arc.

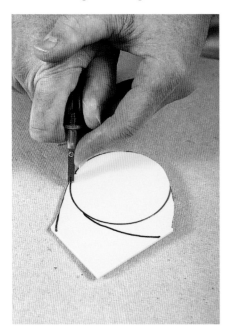

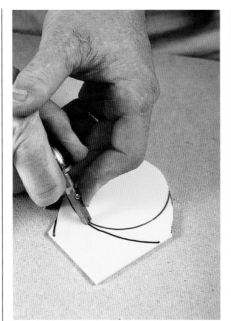

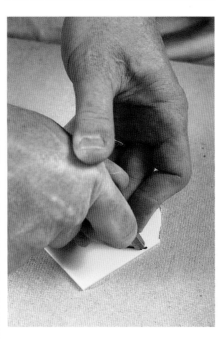

Break the glass along the score.

Continue scoring the glass and breaking it.

The last score you make will take care of the small bit of glass remaining.

Remove the piece with pliers.

The three shapes you just cut represent the basic kinds of pieces you will deal with when making the projects in this book. If you want more practice with shapes, just transfer the following patterns onto scrap pieces of glass and cut them as numbered.

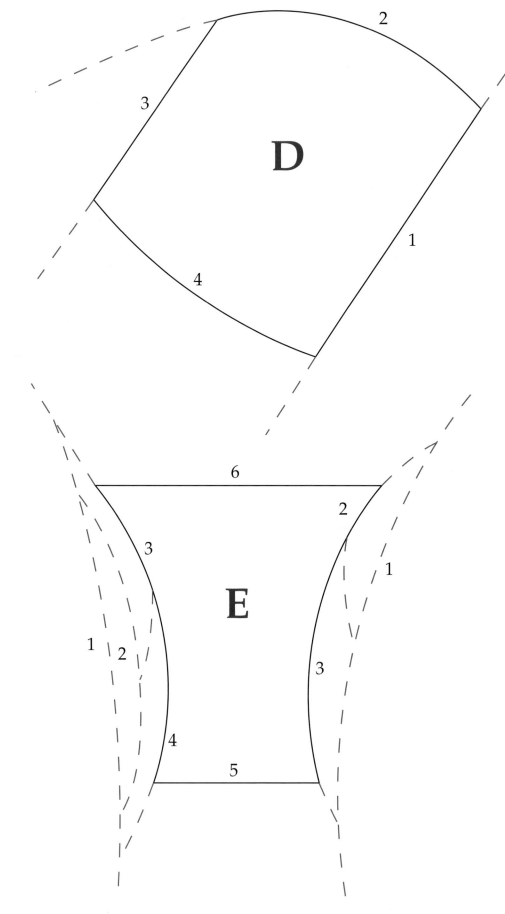

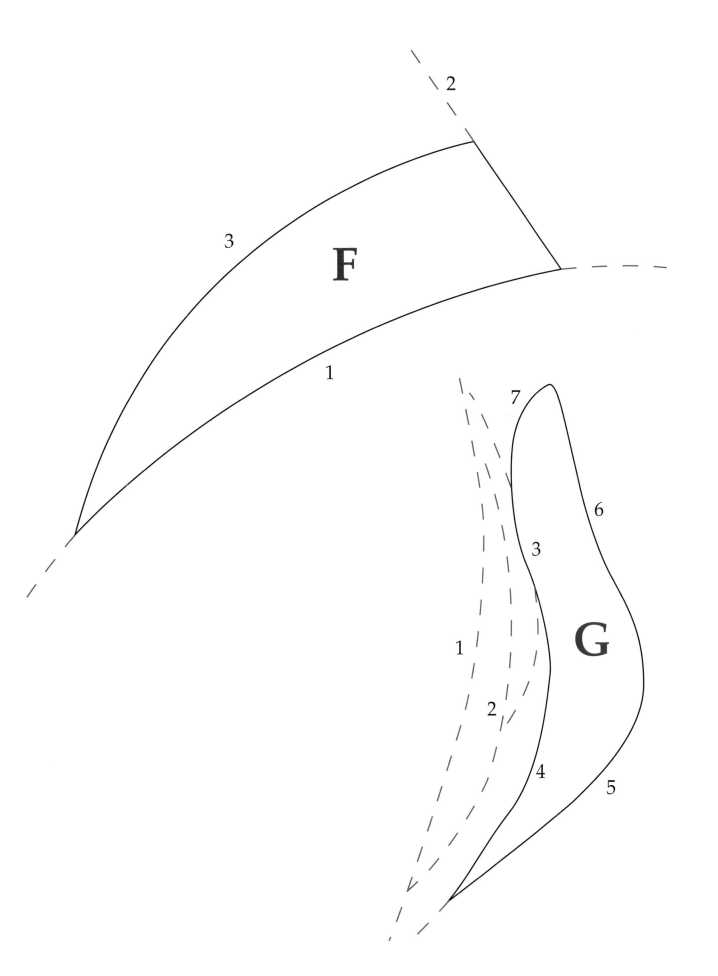

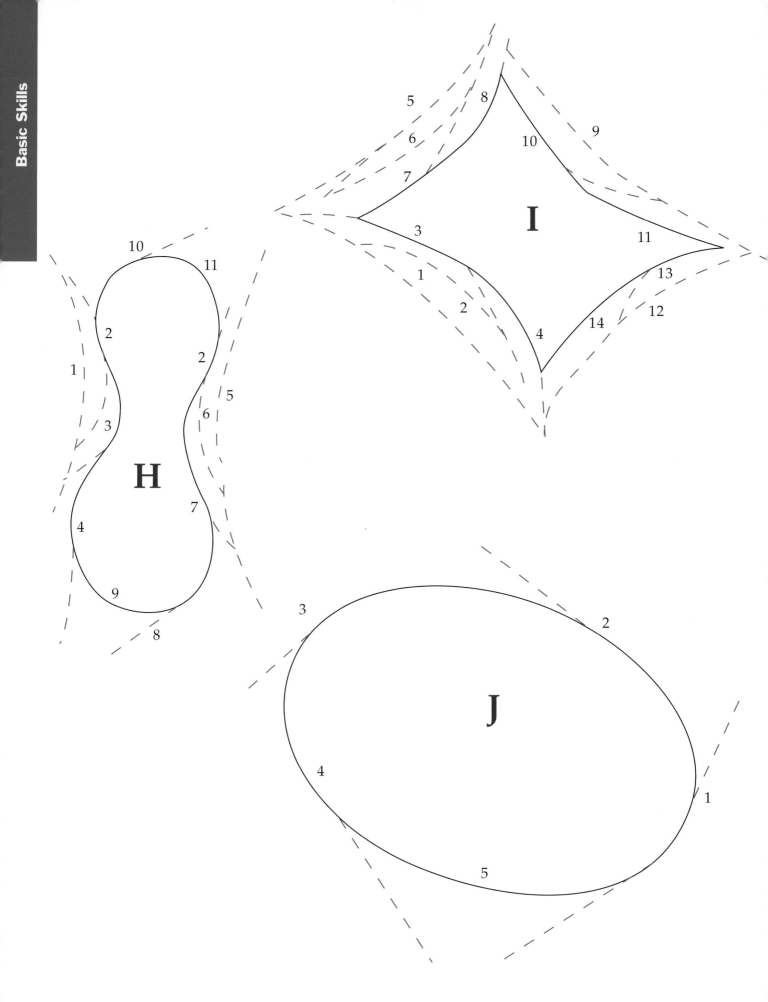

Grozing

You will notice that the edges of the pieces you have cut are somewhat rough and jagged. These excess "burrs" of glass need to be removed using a process called grozing, in which you use pliers to bite away unwanted edges of glass.

The indented curve drawn here for illustrative purposes simulates an unwanted lip of glass that grozing pliers can remove.

Position the pliers so that a corner of the jaws is pressed on the first $1/4$ inch or so of the edge you want to work on.

If you are using pliers that are designed for both grozing and breaking, you must make sure to hold them in the proper way, with the curved jaw at the top. The jaws should be perpendicular when gripping the glass to break pieces.

Apply pressure to the handles of the tool; the jaws will bite into the glass and you will hear a gritty, crunching sound. While gripping the glass, bring the pliers away from the glass in a short snapping motion—almost like a bird pecking quickly. This will help detached shards fall away from the piece as you work.

Continue grozing until all of the burrs are removed.

After grozing, you should grind the edges of each piece for greater smoothness and evenness.

Grinding

If you are grinding by hand, make sure the Carborundum stone is moistened with water to reduce friction.

Press the grinding stone securely against the rough edge and scrape it along the glass in a fluid motion away from you, much like sanding a piece of wood with sandpaper. The hard stone will strip away layers of glass, leaving a smooth surface. It will generally take a few passes with the stone to remove all of the unwanted burrs and rough spots.

If you plan to make a lot of stained glass projects, a motorized grinding wheel is a good investment that will save you time. It works using the same concept as the grinding stone, except this method uses a spinning wheel covered in coarse diamond to smooth rough edges of glass. These tabletop grinders can be somewhat pricey. You must read all of the instructions provided by the manufacturer before beginning. Remember to always wear eye protection, and make sure there is enough water in the reservoir to keep the wheel moist.

Place an unfinished piece of glass on the grinder and carefully press the edge of the glass against the spinning wheel.

You don't have to apply much pressure for the grinding wheel to polish the glass quickly. Make sure you smooth each edge evenly; use care so corners that are supposed to be sharp and pointy are not blunted off.

When using a tabletop grinder around a template, don't take off so much glass that you begin stripping away paper. If you do, there is a good chance the finished piece won't fit properly with the others when you try to assemble the project.

Go ahead and grind all of the rough edges on your practice pieces until they are smooth. Then rinse them with detergent to remove glass dust.

Applying Copper Foil

Copper foil (see page 9) must be applied to the edges of glass pieces that will be soldered together. The metal in the foil provides the surface the melted solder needs to adhere properly and hold two or more pieces together.

Virtually all copper foil sold is backed by adhesive material like that found on tape. Once this backing is peeled off, the foil is ready to be stuck onto the edge of the glass. The sticky side of the foil is usually either copper-colored like the topside, or black. The black-bottom foil is used on pieces of glass that are very transparent or mirrored, when you can see clearly through the glass to the edge. The foil helps to deaden unwanted reflections in this way. Choose a thickness of foil based on the thickness of the glass as well as the aesthetic qualities of the piece. For example, a project that calls for very delicate lines would most likely need a thin foil, while a bolder, rugged work might require the sturdy look of a thicker foil.

Foil can be applied either by hand or with the help of a foiling machine, which is much like a tape dispenser and can save time if you plan to make a large number of stained glass projects. Both methods are relatively easy to learn.

Begin by peeling the backing away from the foil.

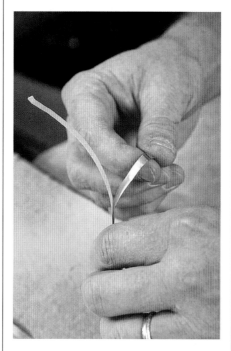

Start applying the foil at the midpoint of one of the sides, not at a corner edge, where it might have difficulty sticking and be easily peeled away.

Keep the strand of foil under a bit of tension by pulling it as you press the adhesive against the edge, turning the piece as you work. Keep the foil centered on the edge, so an equal amount of it hangs over each side. It will be pressed into place a little later.

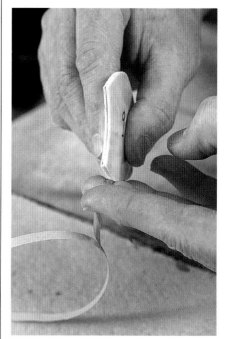

If you notice that the foil has been applied unevenly, simply peel it off and reapply it so that it is straight. Don't peel and reapply the same piece of foiling more than a few times, or the adhesive may lose its stickiness.

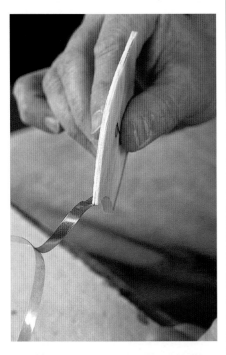

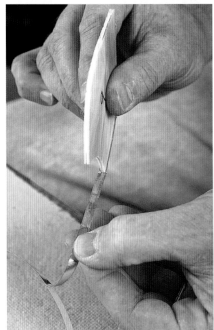

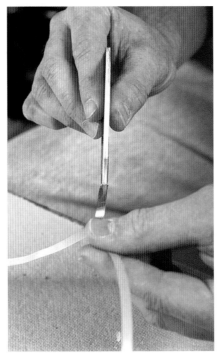

Continue foiling around the entire edge of the piece until you reach the starting point of the foil. Overlap the front and back ends of the foil slightly.

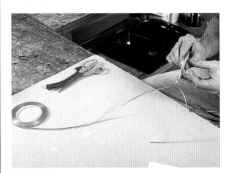

Trim the foil.

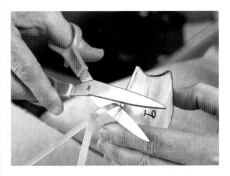

46

Carefully fold down the over-hanging edges so they stick to the glass.

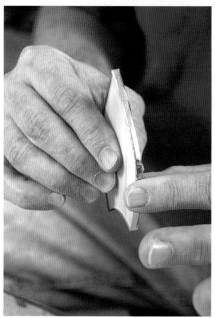

Applying pressure with your thumb and forefinger works well.

Corners can be a little tricky at first.

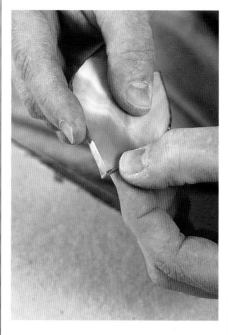

The best approach is to square off the edges where they meet at the corner, in much the same manner as presents are wrapped. This is also known as "hospital corners" when making a bed.

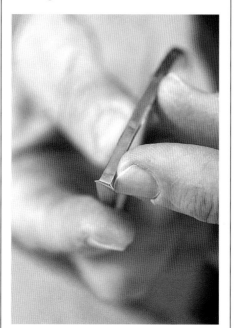

These raised edges need to be folded down flat.

Make sure the foil is firmly pressed down all the way around the piece.

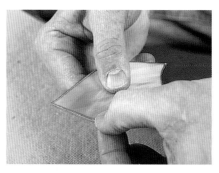

The process is the same when using thicker foil, as shown here. Make sure the foil remains centered.

Corners present an even bigger challenge when the foil is thick.

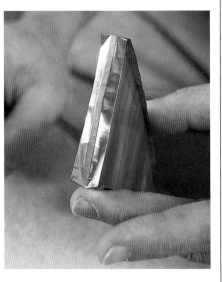

Press the edges of the foil down so two folds meet at the corner.

Press one of these folds until it is flat.

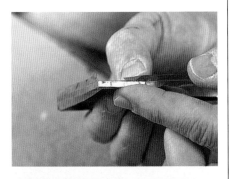

Repeat on the other side.

A foiling machine gives a bit more control over the foil because it is dispensed off the spool evenly. The foil must first be peeled away from its paper backing and threaded correctly in the machine; read all of the instructional materials provided by the manufacturer.

Begin foiling at a midway point on one of the sides and apply evenly around the entire edge of the piece. Make sure the foil stays centered on the edge of the glass, so that equal sections of foil hang over either side.

Make sure to leave a small overlap where the front end of the foil meets the back end. Cut the foil with scissors.

Press down any raised areas you see around the edge of the foil.

When you have finished pressing down the foil, it is time to burnish it. A wooden or plastic burnishing tool, also called a fid, will work well. They come in many shapes and sizes.

Press down on the edge of the foil firmly and slide the fid across it until all bumps are gone.

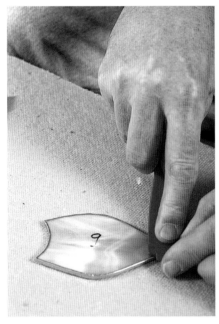

Your piece should look like this when it is finished.

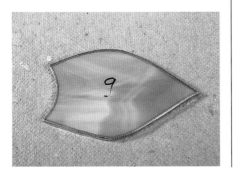

Basic Foil Repair

Sometimes a less-than-perfect foiling job can be salvaged with a few modifications using a craft knife.

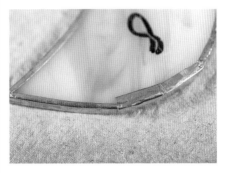

Trim the excess foil evenly along the edge.

Use the tip of the knife to peel away the excess foil.

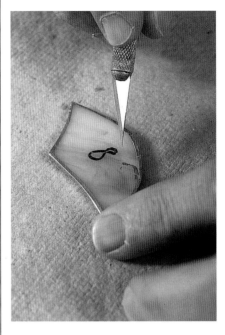

Keep in mind that some uneven foiling jobs cannot be fixed with this method. In those cases, the only solution is to peel off the foil and start over.

6

Foiled Glass Panel

Time investment: 6–8 hours total

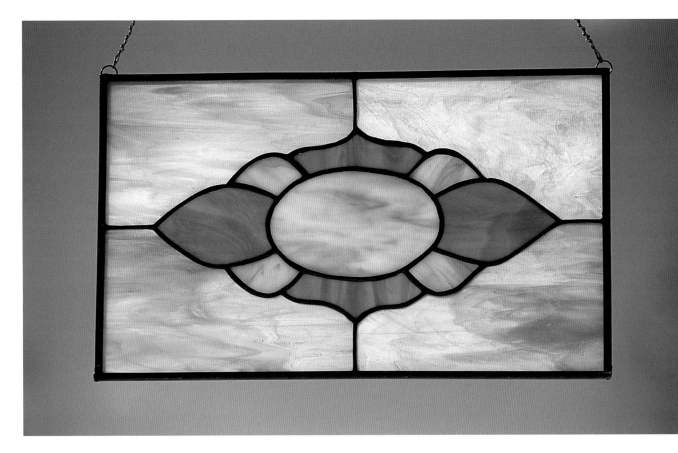

So far you have practiced scoring glass to achieve different shapes and curves, you have grinded glass to smooth it, and you have become comfortable applying copper foil to edges of cut pieces of stained glass. It's now time to put those new skills to use on your first complete project: a foiled glass panel.

In doing this project you will also learn techniques for making and cutting out a paper pattern and template; soldering pieces of glass together with a soldering iron; adding a lead border; and attaching hardware needed to hang the piece when it is finished.

This panel, also called a "window" by hobbyists, is a classic that can be hung in front of a regular window so sunlight streams through it and produces a lustrous glow. With a bit of practice and care, you can even build a panel to customized dimensions to fit into an existing window or door, such as a transom.

SHOPPING LIST: Foiled Glass Panel

This project requires a total of about 1 square foot of glass for each of the four different colors. Please note that glass estimates factor in some excess material to allow for a few mistakes.

Item		Quantity
❑ Glass cutter	(pages 3–4)	
❑ Cutting oil	(page 4)	One bottle
❑ Soldering iron	(page 5)	
❑ Solder	(page 5)	One spool
❑ Flux	(page 6)	One bottle
❑ Flux brush	(page 6)	
❑ Ruler	(page 6)	
❑ Pattern shears	(page 7)	
❑ Grozing/breaking pliers	(page 7)	
❑ Needle-nose pliers	(page 8)	
❑ Carborundum stone	(page 8)	
❑ Copper foil	(page 9)	One spool
❑ Lead came	(page 10)	A strip at least 6 feet long
❑ Lead cutters	(page 11)	
❑ Horseshoe nails	(page 11)	About a dozen
❑ Safety goggles	(page 11)	
❑ Lead board	(page 12)	
❑ Wooden or plastic fid	(page 13)	
❑ Patina	(page 14)	One bottle
❑ Rubber gloves	(page 14)	
❑ Paper towels/cleaning rag	(page 15)	
❑ Flux remover	(page 14)	
❑ Finishing compound	(page 14)	One bottle
❑ Carbon paper	(page 16)	At least one large sheet
❑ Oak tag	(page 16)	At least one large sheet
❑ Tracing paper	(page 16)	At least one large sheet
❑ Plastic basin and sponge	(page 15)	
❑ Thumbtacks and jig material	(page 15)	One complete kit
❑ Rubber cement	(page 16)	One bottle
❑ Colored pencils	(page 16)	
❑ Dustpan and brush	(page 11)	

If you have difficulty locating materials or equipment in your local craft store or stained glass shop, you can find them easily on the Internet. All of the items needed to make the projects in this book can be found at www.rainbowvisionsg.com, or you can log on to your favorite search engine and type "stained glass making" + "supplies" to contact hundreds of other online retailers.

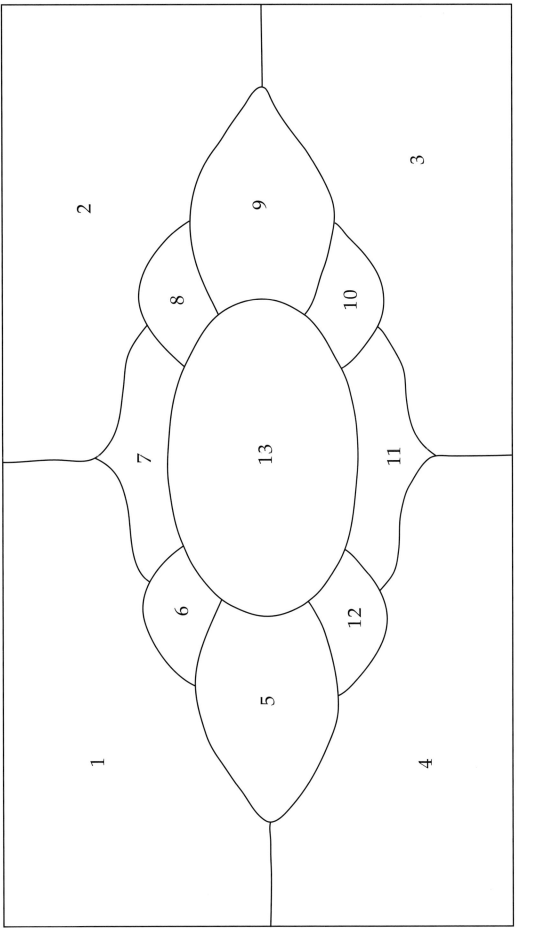

Enlarge 165%

1. Place the pattern from this book on a copier and enlarge by the recommended percentage.

2. Next, you will need three additional sheets of paper, each measuring roughly 24 by 18 inches: 1) a sheet of heavy-stock paper, much like the oak tag paper used in business folders, which will be used as the pattern upon which the project is built; 2) a piece of carbon paper, which will transfer the photocopied pattern when you trace on it; and 3) a piece of tracing paper, which will be used for the templates that are glued to the glass before cutting.

3. You need to arrange the different kinds of paper in the proper order to make a good copy. Make sure the heavy-stock paper is on the bottom of the stack with the carbon paper on top of it, followed by the photocopied pattern and the tracing paper on the very top.

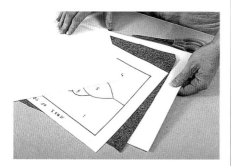

4. Place a Homasote board or preferred surface on your work area. Arrange the papers so they are even, with the pattern directly in the center. Use tacks to hold down the corners of the papers.

5. Begin tracing the pattern. Because this particular pattern uses straight lines to form a rectangle along the outside edges, use a ruler for accuracy. Use a ballpoint pen or other writing instrument with a hard tip for tracing; keep in mind that you must press down firmly on the top layer of tracing paper, leaving enough of an impression to transfer the pattern's image through the carbon paper and onto the heavy paper on the bottom. Felt-tipped markers are not recommended because they typically are too soft to leave the needed impression.

6. Continue carefully tracing the lines. Very slight alterations from the original pattern will not affect the project, but you should retrace the pattern if lines appear to be off by more than a $1/4$ inch or so.

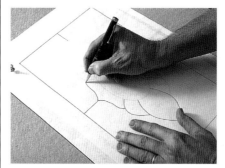

7. When you finish tracing, number each separate piece of the project. This will help to avoid confusion later on with pieces of similar shapes. Use a numbering system that you find logical and easy to understand, such as a clockwise one.

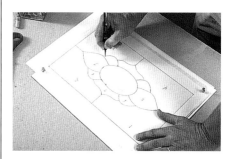

8. Use a pair of regular household scissors to trim excess paper from the edges of the pattern.

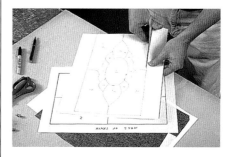

9. Switch to a pair of pattern shears designed for foiled glass projects to cut out all of the other pieces.

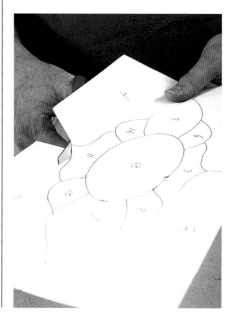

10. Pattern shears for foil projects remove a strip of paper $1/32$ inch wide, a space allowance that will accommodate the foil used to hold pieces of stained glass together. Finish cutting out the shapes from the pattern.

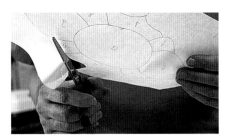

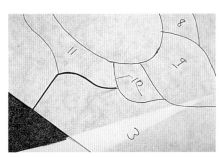

11. It is a good idea to reassemble the pieces of the pattern to make sure they were cut out accurately with no wide gaps between pieces.

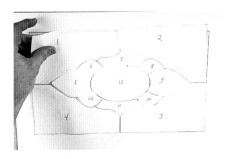

12. Use colored pencils to mark an arrow on each piece to indicate the direction you want the pattern or texture in the stained glass to run on the project.

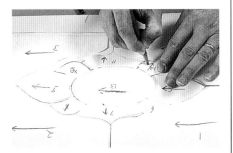

13. Use rubber cement to glue each paper shape onto the stained glass sheets you have chosen.

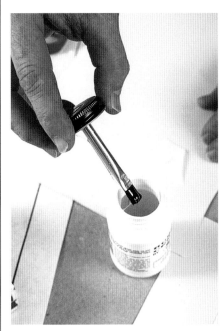

14. Make sure you follow the arrows regarding the direction of the pattern or texture in the stained glass.

15. Arrange pieces on the stained glass to reduce unnecessary waste.

16. With the four bigger corner pieces, use a full sheet of stained glass and take advantage of the right-angle corners already present.

This will save you a lot of meticulous cutting!

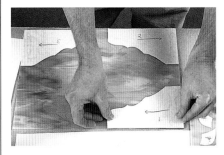

17. Begin cutting out the pieces with your glass cutter. Score the big sheet of glass down the middle and separate it into two pieces.

18. Score the middle of each half and separate them into two pieces.

19. The first cut on this piece will remove excess glass; the marking pen is used here for illustration purposes, but beginners are encouraged to draw their own lines and cut along them for accuracy.

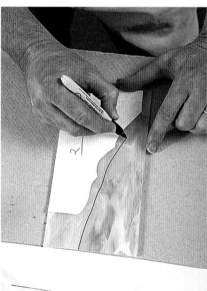

20. Score the line you drew and remove the excess glass.

21. Cut the middle curve next. Draw an arc about one-third of the way into the curve.

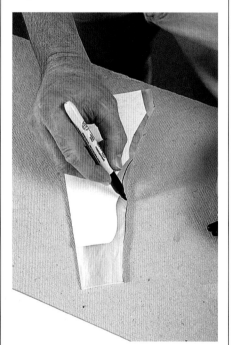

22. Score the arc with your cutter. Remember to cut off small amounts of glass at a time rather than large hunks.

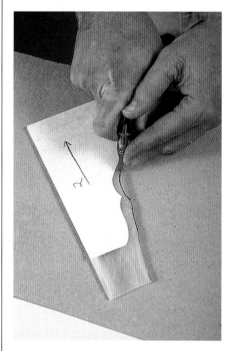

23. Snap it free with breaking pliers.

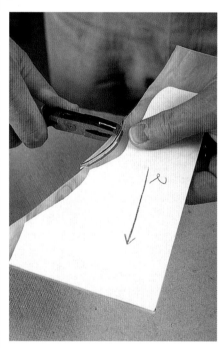

24. Draw another line about halfway into the curve and score it with your cutter.

25. Snap that piece loose.

26. Score the final arc of the middle curve; because the paper on the pattern gives you an obvious edge to follow, there is no need to draw that arc with a marker.

27. Snap the last hunk free.

28. Score the remaining edges of the piece and remove the excess glass.

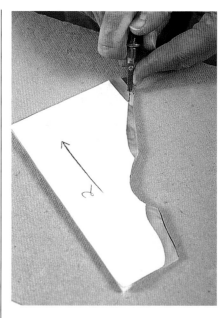

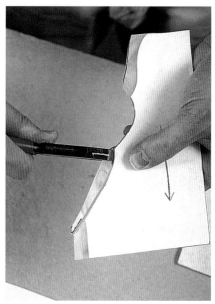

29. Use grozing pliers to gnaw away at any large jagged pieces of glass you see along the edge. Keep in mind that a quick biting motion with the pliers produces good results.

30. Finish the piece by using a handheld grinding stone or a tabletop grinder to smooth the edges of the glass. Use the paper pattern as your guide for deciding how much glass to remove during grinding; don't remove more than extends beyond the paper at any point.

31. Continue cutting out and grinding the rest of the pieces that will be used to make the glass panel.

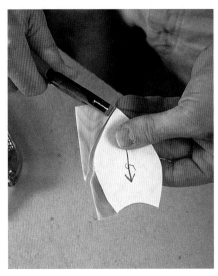

32. Place the heavy-stock pattern on a table and arrange each of the glass pieces on top of it like a puzzle. This is the time to make sure the gaps between the pieces look uniform. Regrind any pieces that do not look uniform.

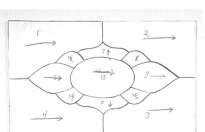

33. Peel the paper pattern from a piece of glass.

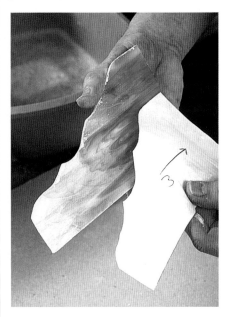

34. Rinse the piece off in warm, soapy water to remove glass shards, dust, and rubber cement.

35. Use a towel to dry it.

36. Immediately renumber the glass and place it in its correct spot on the pattern.

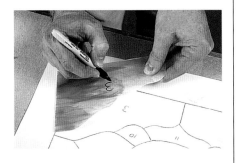

37. Do the same for the remaining pieces.

38. Apply adhesive-backed foil to each of the pieces. Make sure to flatten and smooth the foil with a burnishing tool as your final step with foiling. (See pages 45–49 for tips on proper foiling.)

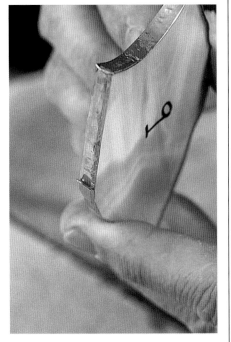

39. Arrange all of the foiled pieces in their correct places on top of the pattern; butt four pieces of jig material firmly against each edge of the panel. Secure them with tacks or pushpins.

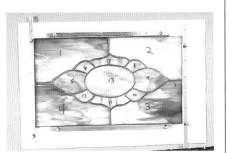

40. You will next need to tack solder the pieces that compose the panel. Tack soldering involves applying a small amount of molten solder to various spots to hold the pieces together temporarily while working on the project.

41. Plug in your soldering iron and allow it to heat up. For safety, remember to place the iron in its holder when not in use.

42. Before you begin soldering, experiment a little to find a comfortable grip to use on the iron. Some people prefer a grip similar to the one used to hold a pencil.

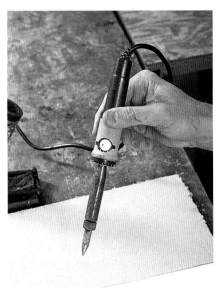

Others find a "flashlight" style grip to be more to their liking. Perhaps a combination of grips will suit you, depending on your needs. You will become more comfortable with the iron the more you try soldering.

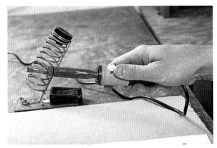

- You must apply flux to all metal surfaces before soldering. If the solder refuses to melt and flow properly, and instead forms heaps or mounds on your project, you probably forgot the flux. Just apply some and continue soldering.
- Frequently drag the tip of the soldering iron across a damp sponge or cloth to remove built-up solder and flux residue. Especially keep this in mind after you finish soldering a long seam or a number of smaller spots.
- Try not to lean directly over the spot where the raw solder meets the hot iron; the fumes emitted contain toxins.
- An iron that is not hot enough will cause the solder to blob up and refuse to flow properly.
- An iron that is too hot will cause the solder to flow too quickly, and it may transfer too much heat through the copper foil, causing the glass to crack.

- Also be careful using an overly hot iron around lead, because it will turn it to slag in an instant.

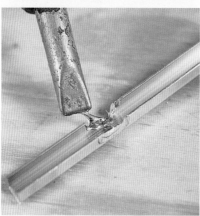

- Gauging the proper temperature for a soldering iron is tricky. An effective and quick test: Touch the hot iron to a cool bead of solder. If it turns to liquid instantly and stays attached to the iron, the temperature is good.

43. Use a small brush to apply flux to all of the foiled edges of the pieces. Flux removes oxidation and other dirt from the metal surfaces in preparation for soldering. Solder will not bond with metal unless flux is applied to the metal first.

44. Apply the flux liberally to the foil, using a painting motion. Don't worry about getting flux on the glass—it will not harm it in any way. Soldering must be done within a few minutes of the application of flux, otherwise the flux might evaporate and make soldering difficult if not impossible. Should this occur, simply apply more flux and continue.

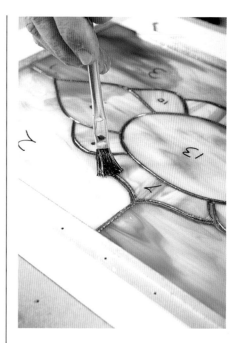

45. Make sure the tip of the iron is clean if it is not brand new.

46. If not, use a moistened sponge to remove debris, or rub the heated tip across a block of sal ammoniac to remove a more substantial buildup. (See page 6 for more information about sal ammoniac).

47. Unspool a strand of solder, making sure it is long enough for you to handle comfortably when reaching the different areas of the project. Peel off more as needed while soldering.

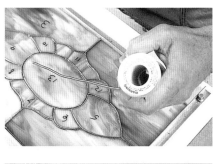

48. To tack solder, you simply place the tip of the solder wire against the copper foil where you intend to solder it, then touch the hot iron to the solder quickly—no more than a few seconds—to melt a small amount of it. If you hold the soldering iron in one place for too long, the heat might crack the glass.

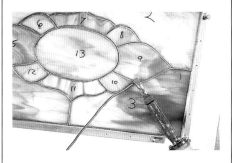

49. Lift the soldering iron a short distance to allow the molten solder to flow onto the foiled pieces. It will cool almost immediately, holding the pieces together.

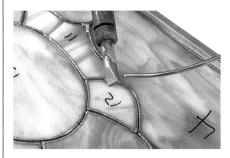

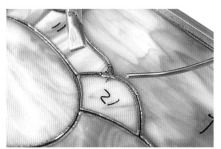

50. Tack solder the panel wherever two or more seams intersect. This will hold your project together as you work on it.

51. Remove the framing material from around the project. Your piece should look similar to this:

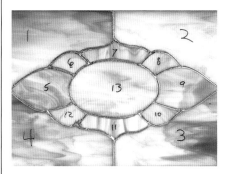

52. You are now ready to solder the seams. This is perhaps the trickiest technique you will encounter during soldering, and it will take a little trial and error to get it right.

Soldering along seams involves a set of two different steps: applying a proper amount of solder to a fluxed area of copper foil or lead, and then smoothing it out along the seam to form a slightly raised line of solder called a bead.

53. The real challenge is finding the right speed to move the soldering iron and solder when melting it onto the foil. Once you develop a feel for that, the technique becomes much easier. Position the end of the solder and the tip of the iron near each other over the end of the foiled seam you intend to work on; the iron should be at a 45-degree angle to the foil. Gently touch the tip of the solder and the iron together for an instant and remove a 1/4-inch hunk of solder. Don't hold the solder against the iron for more than a second, or too much solder will melt. Let the solder flow onto the foil, pulling the iron toward you at a speed that allows the solder to adequately cover the foil. Lift the iron straight up from the solder without brushing forward or backward, as this will create lumps and uneven spots in the bead. Like water, solder will naturally find its level point, leaving a nice smooth and shiny finish when it cools.

54. If the solder you added fails to completely cover the foil, melt more solder to the bead. If you apply too much solder, simply use the tip of the iron to peck away and remove solder from the very end of the bead. As an alternative, you can tilt the seam, heat the solder, and allow it to flow off the piece and onto your work surface. Be careful to avoid the falling drops of molten solder. They will burn you instantly!

55. Immediately reposition the tip of the iron and the tip of the solder wire over the next section of exposed copper foil, remove a 1/4-inch hunk of solder, and touch it to the seam. Again, allow the solder to flow unobstructed and remove the iron by pulling it straight up. This new line of solder will flow and join the first seam you applied.

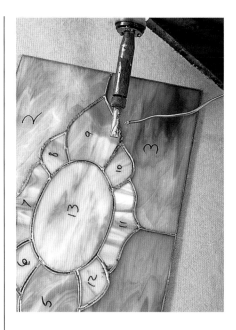

56. Continue soldering the foil seams between the pieces. Your timing and your movements will become more fluid as you get comfortable with the process, and your beads will form nicely.

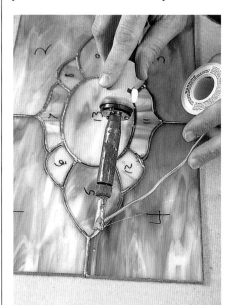

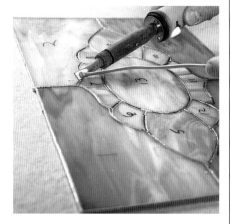

57. As you work your way around the piece, you will encounter cooled areas of solder you applied earlier. To make the old and new solder flow together seamlessly at their junction, touch your iron onto the end of the cooled solder to heat it. Immediately apply the new solder to the foil and allow it to flow smoothly to join up with the other solder.

58. Don't worry if some stray drops of solder splash onto the glass and harden. It can be removed very easily with a scraper when cooled.

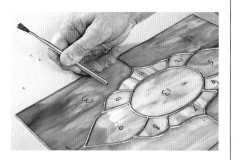

Although you could apply solder along the outside foil edges of the project to finish it, we will instead be adding lead cames as a more decorative border.

59. When you have soldered all the inside seams, your project will look like this. Don't worry about uneven sections of solder beads at this point; there will be time to smooth them later.

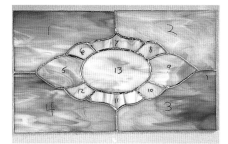

60. Turn the panel over so the reverse side faces up.

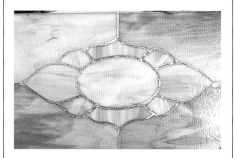

61. Apply flux to all copper foil seams.

62. It's now time to solder all of the seams of this side.

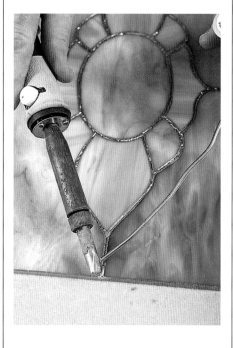

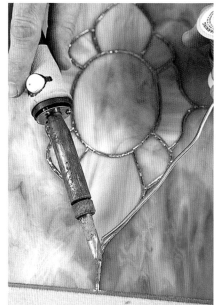

63. Make sure you don't hold the soldering iron in one spot for more than about a second because it might overheat the foil and cause the solder on the underside of the panel to remelt. This will cause the solder on the top side of the panel to become indented.

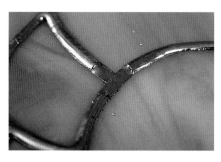

Additionally, a large mound or blob of solder will form at the same spot on the opposite side.

64. This unsightly mound of solder—and any other irregular contours along the seam—can be corrected by gently touching the hot iron to the blemish and holding it there for an instant. This will cause the solder to melt and flow evenly.

Repeat this process as needed on both sides of the project.

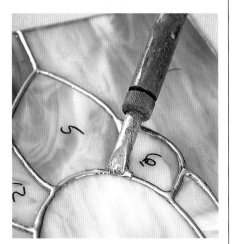

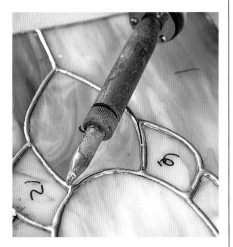

65. Make sure the foiled outer edges of the project are free of solder, particularly where a seam meets the edge. The lead cames (see page 10) that will be used as a border on this project need to fit snugly against the foil.

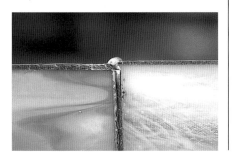

66. Remove any pieces of solder you find by touching them with the soldering iron.

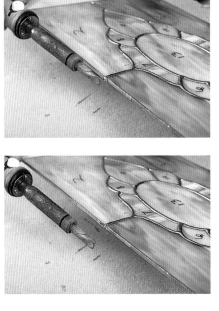

67. Get a piece of U-shaped lead came that is 5 or 6 feet in length.

68. In its original form, lead came is very supple and wiggly. It must be stretched before use. Stick one end of the came into a lead vise.

69. Grab the opposite end with a pair of pliers and, working across a tabletop or other supporting surface, tug on the came in a series of quick jerks. This action will remove the waviness from the came and help to make it firmer.

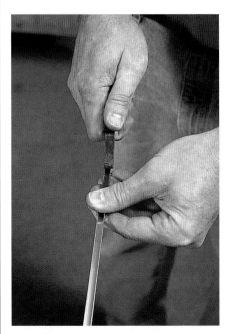

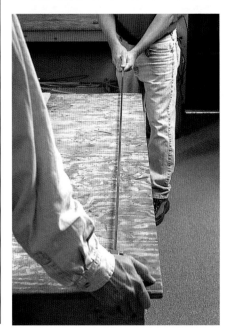

Depending on the design of your lead vise, you might need an assistant to hold the end of the lead came so it doesn't slip while you stretch it.

70. Measure the bottom edge of the panel, and mark a spot about an inch beyond the right edge. Here the measurement falls at the 15-inch mark.

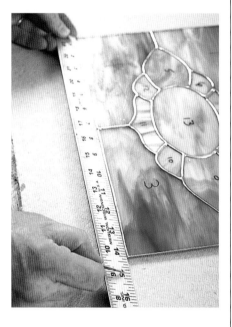

71. Scratch a line in the lead at the 15-inch mark.

Check to make sure the end of the came is not crumpled or bent.

If it is, simply trim off a small bit with lead pliers or a lead knife until you have a straight cut.

72. Now cut the came at the line you marked with lead pliers or a lead knife.

73. Place a lead board onto your work surface, and set the glass panel on the lead board. Make sure to have a hammer and a handful of horseshoe nails within easy reach. They will be used in a few moments.

74. Put the piece of lead came against the inside bottom edge of the board, with the U-shaped channel facing toward the project.

75. Slide the edge of the glass into the channel. Press it firmly so that it is seated in the channel properly.

76. Leave a slight gap of about $\frac{1}{2}$ inch along the right angle of the lead board. Another piece of came will be placed along the edge in the next several steps.

77. Measure the left side of the panel and scratch a mark into the came at the spot where the cames meet and cut the piece.

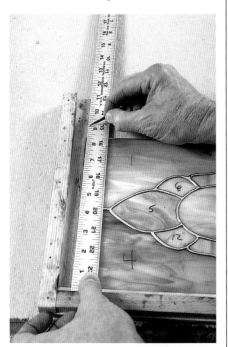

78. Place the came against the side of the lead board with the U-shaped channel facing toward the project.

79. Adjust the glass panel until it fits into the channel, making sure the glass remains in the bottom piece of came as well.

80. The cames will form a right angle in the lower left corner of the project, as shown.

81. Measure the right side of the panel, cut a piece of came, and adjust the panel until the right edge sits inside the channel.

82. Secure the came in place. Beginning at the bottom right corner, tap a horseshoe nail into the wood so it is flush with the outside edge of the came; repeat this twice more at intervals of about 4 inches or so. Be careful not to drive the nail into the came!

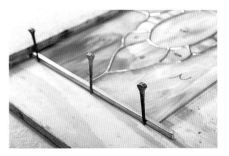

83. Measure the top edge of the panel.

84. Scratch a mark into the came at the spot where the cames will meet and cut that section off with lead pliers.

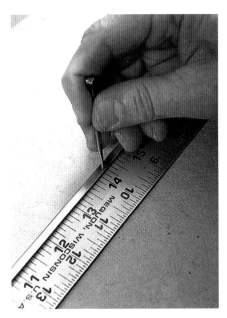

85. Fit this section between the ends of the two pieces of came on either side and, if necessary, trim it to fit snugly between them.

86. Use three evenly spaced horseshoe nails to secure this piece of came.

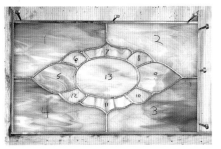

87. Apply flux to the spot where the came meets the solder on the panel in the top center of the piece.

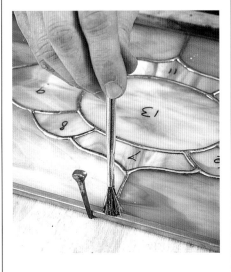

88. Apply solder to that spot to secure the came to the panel. Please note that soldering lead came requires a lower temperature for the iron than soldering copper foil. The temperature of the iron is correct if you can touch it to a scrap of lead for 3 seconds without melting it.

89. Repeat this process at the three other midpoint spots on each side of the panel and at all four corners.

90. The panel will now be held together well enough to handle. Remove the horseshoe nails.

91. Turn the panel over.

92. Apply flux to the four corners and midpoints on this side of the panel.

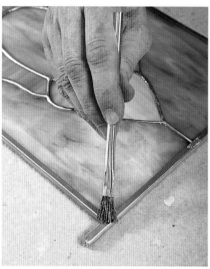

93. Solder these spots.

94. Use lead pliers to snip the excess piece of came flush with the other piece.

95. This will leave a hole exposing the U-channel of the came.

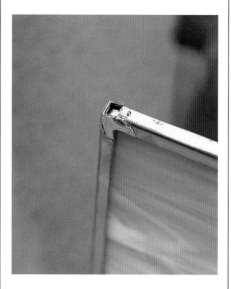

96. Use your soldering iron to pick up and melt about $1/8$ inch of solder wire.

97. Allow the solder to drip into the hole, filling it.

Repeat this process on the other overhanging piece of came.

98. Add hardware to the panel for hanging. (Some people prefer to prop their stained glass panels on a windowsill, while others choose to hang them in front of a sunlit window.)

99. Use a pair of pliers or tweezers to grasp a metal O-ring manufactured for picture hanging. You will need two of these hoops—one each for the upper right and left corners of the panel.

100. Apply flux to the hoop.

101. Hold the hoop near the upper corner, as shown, and solder it into place.

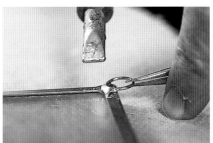

Repeat on the opposite corner.

102. Now fill a basin with warm, soapy water and use a sponge to rub off pen markings and flux residue.

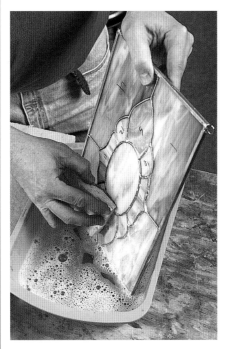

103. Dry with a towel. Cloth towels are a good choice because they are stronger and more absorbent than paper.

104. Apply flux remover and wipe dry.

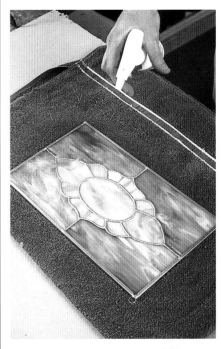

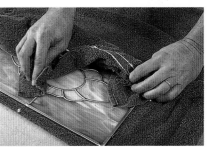

105. Put on a pair of rubber gloves and apply patina to a sponge.

106. Run the sponge along the lead border and all soldered parts of the panel as if you were applying stain to a piece of wood. The patina used for this project darkens the metal portions.

107. Dip the panel in warm, soapy water and wash away excess patina. The darkened part of the metal will not be affected by water. Rinse off the patina under running water.

108. Spray the panel with flux remover and wipe dry.

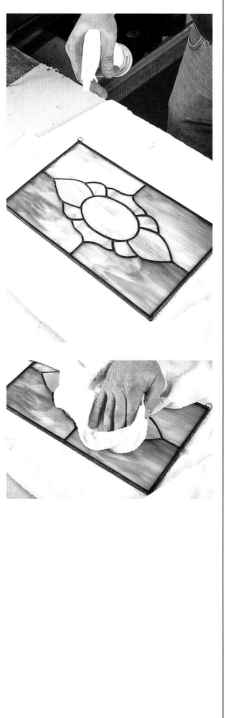

109. Apply finishing compound to the project and buff it until it shines.

7

Lead Came Panel

Time investment: About 6–8 hours total

The skills you learned making the copper foil project in the previous section will serve you well when you make this lead came panel—the most traditional of all stained glass projects.

Instead of long beads of solder, lead cames are used to hold together the pieces of glass in this project. When the glass and lead are assembled correctly, the cames are then soldered to secure them. Once soldered, the glass and lead must be coated in glazing cement to seal them into place.

This process mirrors techniques that are hundreds of years old and represents the cornerstone of the craft. For the example created here, glass was selected that radiated warm, understated tones for a nostalgic feeling.

This project requires a total of about 1 square foot of glass for each of the the three different colors; you will also need a jewel piece of glass with a 1-inch diameter. Please note that glass estimates factor in some excess material to allow for a few mistakes.

Item		Quantity
❏ Glass cutter	(pages 3–4)	
❏ Cutting oil	(page 4)	One bottle
❏ Soldering iron	(page 5)	
❏ Solder	(page 5)	One spool
❏ Flux	(page 6)	One bottle
❏ Flux brush	(page 6)	
❏ Ruler	(page 6)	
❏ Pattern shears	(page 7)	
❏ Grozing/breaking pliers	(page 7)	
❏ Needle-nose pliers	(page 8)	
❏ Carborundum stone	(page 8)	
❏ Rubber mallet	(page 8)	
❏ Stiff-bristle brush	(page 13)	
❏ Lead came	(page 10)	One 6-foot strip of $1/4$-inch U-channel, and two 6-foot strips of $3/16$-inch H-channel
❏ Lead cutters	(page 11)	
❏ Horseshoe nails	(page 11)	About a dozen
❏ Safety goggles	(page 11)	
❏ Lead board	(page 12)	
❏ Wooden or plastic fid	(page 13)	
❏ Glazing cement	(page 13)	
❏ Whiting	(page 13)	
❏ Masking tape	(page 12)	
❏ Carbon paper	(page 16)	At least one large sheet
❏ Oak tag	(page 16)	At least one large sheet
❏ Tracing paper	(page 16)	At least one large sheet
❏ Plastic basin and sponge	(page 15)	
❏ Rubber cement	(page 16)	One bottle
❏ Colored pencils	(page 16)	
❏ Dustpan and brush	(page 11)	

Lead Came Panel

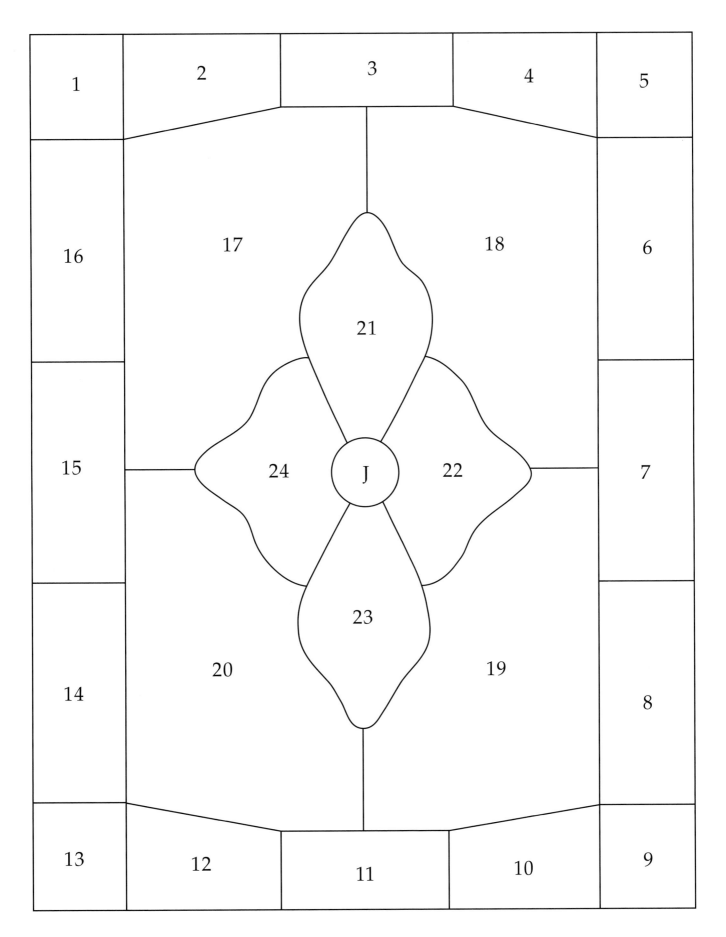

Enlarge 165%

1. Make sure your workspace is clean and free of clutter.

2. Gather the equipment and materials you will need for this project and put them within easy reach.

3. Place a lead board on your work table.

4. Use a copier and enlarge the original pattern in this book by the recommended percentage. A local print shop or office supply store will be able to help you copy the image if you have difficulty.

5. Follow the steps detailed on page 54 for tracing the original to create a pattern on heavy-stock paper.

6. Trim around the edge of the heavy-stock pattern with regular scissors.

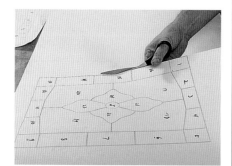

7. Keep in mind that because this project uses lead cames, you must leave a bigger gap between the pieces of glass than with the copper foil project. Make sure you use pattern shears designed for lead projects; if you use pattern shears with an interchangeable center cutting blade, make sure the lead blade is attached. All lead shears will leave a $^1/_{16}$-inch gap between the cut template pieces, perfect to accommodate lead cames.

Use rubber cement to glue all of the template pieces onto the glass sheets you have selected for the project.

8. Use a glass cutter to cut out all of the pieces you will use to make the lead panel. Use grozing pliers to remove obvious jagged spots from the edge of the glass, and then grind the edges until smooth.

9. Peel off the paper templates and wash each piece of glass in a basin of warm, soapy water to remove stray shards of glass and glue. Remember to transfer the number from the paper to the piece of glass with a marking pen after it is dry.

10. Place a piece of lead came along the left and bottom edges, then use one of the pieces of glass and a small scrap of lead came to determine the proper placement for the cames in relation to the sides of the pattern. Keep in mind that the lines shown on the pattern are cut lines, or lines showing where you need to cut the glass. When using lead cames as borders, they will extend beyond the cut line; the same is true for pieces of came used on interior pattern lines between pieces.

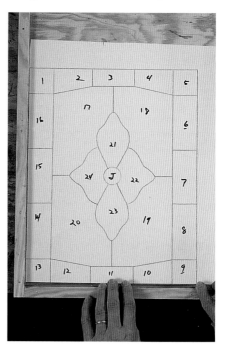

11. Once you have determined the alignment, secure the pattern to the lead board with masking tape along the top and right edges.

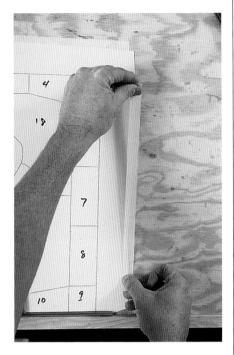

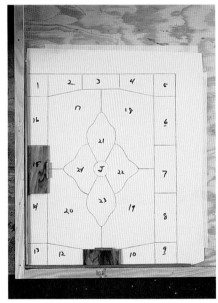

12. Tap a horseshoe nail into the top part of the lead came along the left border. Position the nail so that it pierces the inside edge of the lead came and lodges in the wood of the board. Hammer another horseshoe nail similarly at the right edge of the came along the bottom border.

13. Place the piece labeled "13" into position on the bottom left corner (a portion of the numeral in the photograph as been rubbed away); make sure the left edge and bottom edges of the glass are seated in both channels of the U-channel lead. Place a small scrap piece of H-shaped lead came along the right edge of the piece of stained glass; this is done to simulate the edge where a permanent lead came will be placed a bit later in the project. Now position another piece of H-shaped lead came across the top of the glass, as shown.

14. Scratch a line on this second piece of came to mark the spot where the inside edge of the other came meets it to form a right angle.

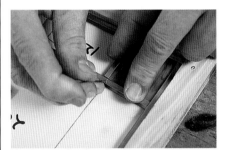

15. Use lead pliers to cut the came at the scratch. Make sure the channel faces up when you cut for the best results.

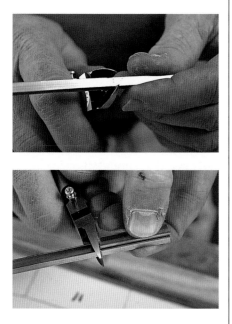

16. Test the piece you just cut to make sure it fits well, as shown.

17. Use the cut piece of came as a guide to cut seven more pieces of H-shaped cames the same length.

18. These will be used between the glass pieces along both the left and right sides of the panel.

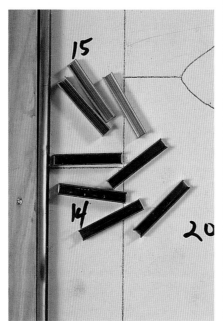

19. Align the glass pieces to form the left edge of the project, as shown; make sure the stained glass pieces are positioned fully in the U-channel of the lead came on the left border, or subsequent pieces will be out of alignment as the project progresses. Place a cut piece of came between each glass piece, making sure the glass is seated firmly in the top and bottom channels of the lead.

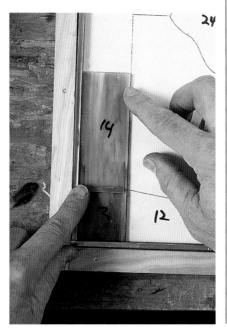

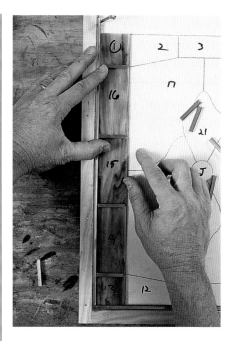

20. Use a horseshoe nail and scrap piece of came along the top edge of the row to hold it in place while you work on the rest of the piece.

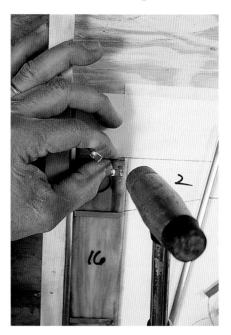

21. Place a strip of H-shaped came along the right edge of the row you just built, making sure that it is slightly longer than the row itself.

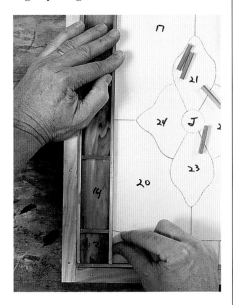

22. Scratch a line on this piece to mark the spot where it meets the came along the top edge to form a right angle.

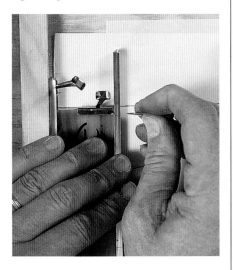

23. Cut the came at the scratch.

The corner should look like this when the came strip is put in place. The pieces will be soldered together later in the project.

24. Hammer two horseshoe nails carefully along the outside right edge of the came strip, near the top and the bottom, to hold it in place.

25. Begin building the bottom border of the project. Place the piece labeled "12" in its correct place. Use a scrap piece of lead came along the top edge of the glass and line up a fresh piece of lead along the right edge, as shown. Mark a line as before and cut the came to make a right angle.

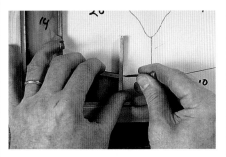

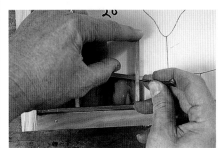

26. Repeat this process with the pieces labeled "11" and "10."

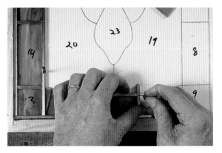

Each came section placed between the pieces of glass should look like this.

27. Use a scrap of lead and a horseshoe nail to hold the bottom row in place.

28. Because the bottom row is designed with a slight curve in it, the lead came that will be placed along the row's top edge must be cut at an angle where it meets the perpendicular came—a straight cut on the came will leave too much of a gap at the junction.

29. Hold the piece of H-shaped came where it meets the piece already in place; scratch a mark in the came to indicate the angle that will be needed for a snug fit. Use lead pliers to cut the came. The two pieces should abut smoothly. Trim the came again if you are not satisfied with the angle.

30. Use a fid to press the lead came into place along the bottom row; press down firmly at the spots where the shorter cames meet.

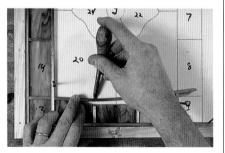

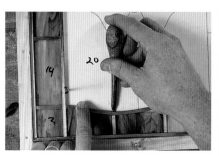

31. When the came is pressed flush, hammer in a horseshoe nail along the top edge at the left side and another one in the center.

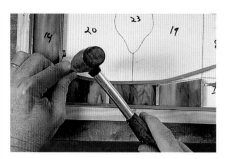

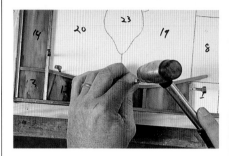

32. Scratch a mark in the came where it intersects with the perpendicular piece at the end of the bottom row. Keep in mind that you must account for the slight angle of the junction when making the mark.

33. Cut the lead along the scratch you just made. Pliers held as shown will work well to lop off the lead, as will a lead knife.

34. Hammer in a horseshoe nail to hold the piece in place.

At this stage, the project will look like this.

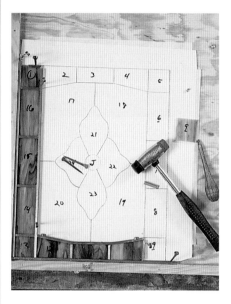

35. Place the large corner piece, here labeled "20," into place. Make sure it fits into the channels of the cames.

78

36. Place a strip of came along the top edge of the piece. Mark it at the top edge of the glass. Notice on the pattern that two other pieces of came will converge on this spot from the right on both the top and bottom; angles must be trimmed into the cames so they fit together well.

37. Cut the piece of came straight across; next, trim each of the four ends of the came at roughly a 45-degree angle. Snip each end firmly. Take a small amount of lead with each snip, and go back later and remove more if needed. The tip will have a pointed appearance.

38. Place the came along the top edge of the piece.

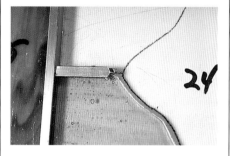

39. Place the piece labeled "17" onto the pattern; use two horseshoe nails and two scrap pieces of came to hold everything in place.

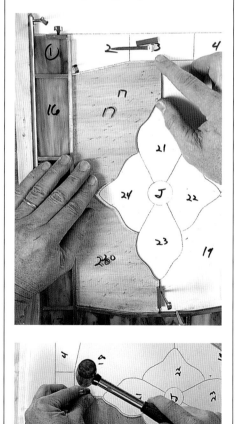

40. Line up a piece of came as shown.

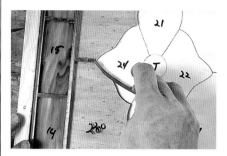

Mark it to indicate the section that needs to be removed for it to fit well with the piece of came that will join it from the top edge.

41. Cut the came along the mark you just made. It should fit as illustrated.

42. Press the came firmly along the edge of the glass until it reaches the point. The angle around the point is too severe to be covered adequately by a single piece of came. Instead, separate pieces need to be cut to keep the lines of lead uniform and sharp.

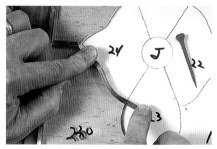

43. Place a scrap piece of came to simulate the border, and scratch a line to indicate where the other piece of came needs to be cut.

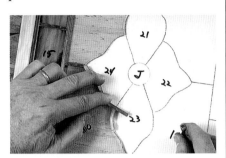

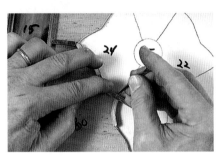

44. Cut the came, and hammer it into place with a horseshoe nail and a scrap piece of came. Repeat this process for the adjoining piece above it.

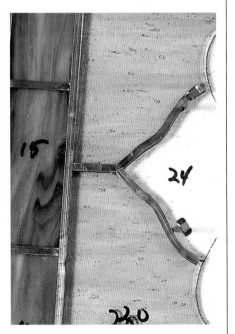

45. When completed, the junction of the three lead cames will look like this.

46. Use a rubber mallet to tap the piece labeled "24" into place as shown.

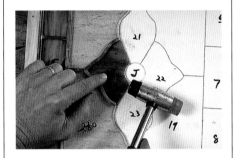

47. Use a horseshoe nail and a scrap piece of came to secure the piece.

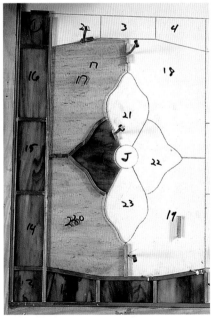

48. Measure and cut pieces of came to fit the left edge of piece "23" and to replace the scrap strip at the bottom right edge of piece "20."

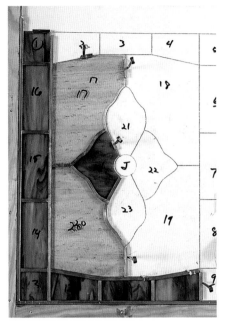

49. Put piece "23" into place and measure and cut a piece of came that will run along its right edge. Use a wooden fid or other hard tool to get the lead to hug inside curves, as shown. Trim the came even with the top edge of the piece. Secure it in place with a horseshoe nail.

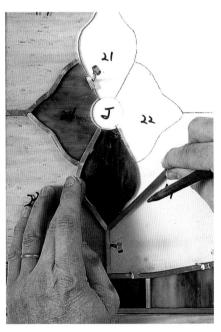

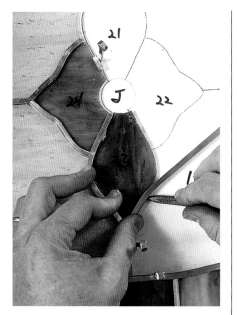

50. Do not try to wrap a single lead came around the tip of pieces such as "23." The curve is too severe, and the lead will gap and buckle when forced in that manner.

Wrong

51. Begin wrapping the round jewel for the center in a piece of H-shaped lead came.

52. Use a wooden fid or other hard tool to press the front edge of the came onto the jewel.

53. Continue bending the came until it overlaps with the front edge.

Scratch a mark where the excess came needs to be cut.

54. Cut the came at the scratch mark with lead pliers.

55. Use a fid to press both ends together.

56. Place the jewel into the center of the pattern. Tap in a horseshoe nail to hold it in place.

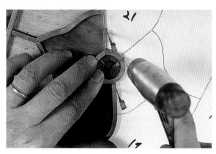

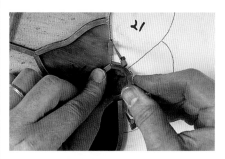

57. Continue building the project, mirroring the steps and techniques you used on the other side.

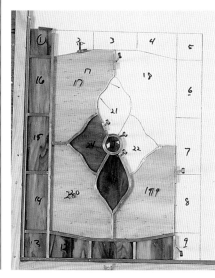

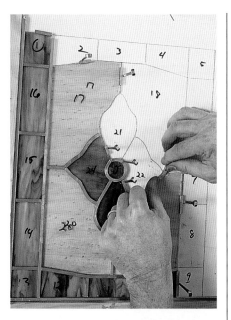

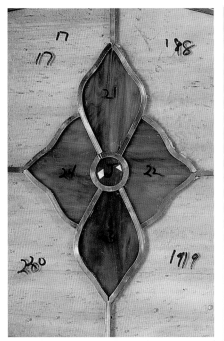

At this stage, the project will look like this:

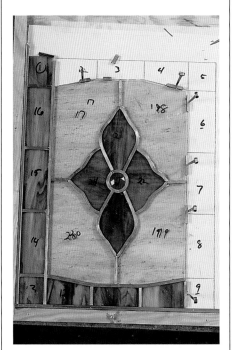

59. Finish building the top row, mirroring the steps and techniques you used to build the bottom row. The order of the pieces will be 2, 3, and 4.

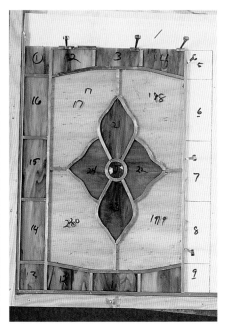

60. Build the right edge in the same manner you built the left.

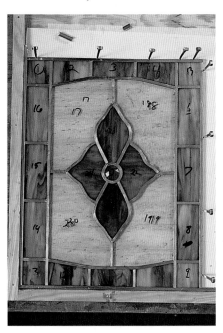

58. The order of the pieces will be 19, 22, 21, and 18 to complete the center of the panel. If you find the actual layout of the panel deviating from the pattern underneath it, stop building and figure out why this is happening. Check to make sure every piece is firmly seated into the cames. If that doesn't solve the problem, one or more of the pieces may need a little more grinding; use your eye and readjust pieces to see where they fall out of alignment.

61. Prepare lead surfaces for tack soldering by applying flux to all of the spots where two or more pieces of lead came meet.

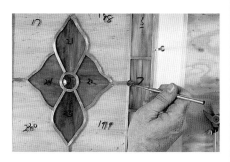

62. Apply about $1/8$ inch of solder at each joint. Use the tip of the soldering iron to allow the solder to flow evenly.

63. Continue doing the same across the rest of the project.

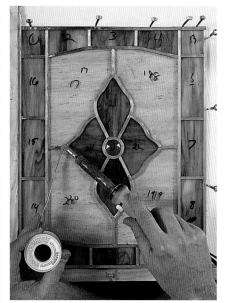

64. If you should encounter an area on the piece where a large gap—more than $1/16$ inch—exists, it must be filled in so solder will adhere to the joint.

65. To do this, snip off a piece of lead came that will fit down in the gap.

Then cut if in half across the horizontal piece of the H.

66. Set it into the gap, and use a pointed tool if needed to help position it properly.

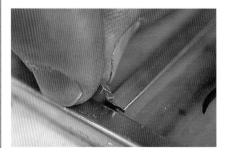

67. Apply flux to the repair.

68. Apply solder to it.

69. When all joints have been soldered, remove the horseshoe nails.

70. Trim off excess came from the border strips.

71. Turn the project over. Apply flux and solder all of the solder joints.

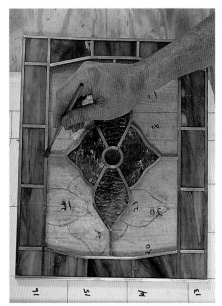

You have probably noticed by now that some of the pieces of stained glass move and rattle around a little within their channels of lead. This is normal and is not a cause for concern, but the panel does need to be glazed or puttied now to make it more durable and to make it weather-resistant if you plan to use it outdoors.

72. Open a container of glazing compound and dump the contents into another container, such as a bowl or coffee can. The compound shown here comes premixed with a liquid designed to thin the compound. Some glazing compounds must be cut with a paint thinner or similar substance so that they can be mixed.

73. Mix the compound until it is the consistency of very thick cake batter.

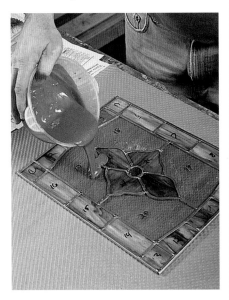

74. Dump roughly a quarter cup of the glazing compound onto one side of the panel.

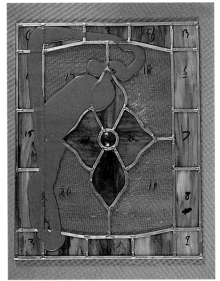

75. Use a very stiff bristle brush to work the compound under the edges of the lead came from all directions. You can vary the motion of the brush from circular to back and forth to ensure complete coverage.

76. Take your time and make sure the compound gets under every seam. Add more compound if necessary.

77. Sprinkle whiting powder, also known as calcium carbonate, liberally across the panel. This powder will help the glazing compound set, and it will help to absorb excess compound from the glass itself.

78. Use your bristle brush and rub the powder vigorously to spread it out and work it into the compound. Brush off excess powder as it becomes moist and clumps. Add more powder if needed to help absorb more of the compound.

79. The finished side will look like this.

80. Turn the project over, apply glazing compound as you did before, and then add whiting powder to absorb it.

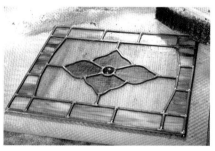

81. The complete project should be allowed to dry for several days at room temperature to allow the compound to set completely.

Should any of the hardened compound work its way out from under the cames, simply use a fid or similar tool to remove it.

8

Tiffany-Style Lampshade

Time investment: About 6–8 hours total

This gorgeous lampshade will serve as the focal point of any room in the house, illuminated as it is by an incandescent bulb that makes the stained glass glisten—giving it a timeless quality that transcends eras.

Patterned after the famed Tiffany style, this project appears at first to be more complex than it actually is. Rest assured that the basics you have learned in this book so far have prepared you to successfully craft this lampshade. The real key to the project is consistency: you must build six identical stained glass panels, and then fasten them together to form a lampshade with pleasing balance and symmetry. Take your time and treat each panel as a separate project, focusing on uniformity in glass cutting, grinding, and soldering.

You will learn a few new techniques in this project as well, such as reinforcing joints with stout wire and adding a lamp base and cap to hold the shade in place properly. Keep in mind that do-it-yourself electrical wiring of any kind is beyond the scope of this book and is not discussed here.

If you plan to display the lamp in a particular room, it is suggested that you choose stained glass colors that will complement the look and feel of the room. A lamp like this can help to accent many types of décor. Take some time to consider what will look appropriate to you.

You will need about 2 square feet of stained glass for the main panel pieces, plus about a square foot each of the two other kinds of glass. Please note that glass estimates factor in some excess material to allow for a few mistakes.

Item		Quantity
❑ Glass cutter	(pages 3–4)	
❑ Cutting oil	(page 4)	One bottle
❑ Soldering iron	(page 5)	
❑ Solder	(page 5)	One spool
❑ Flux	(page 6)	One bottle
❑ Flux brush	(page 6)	
❑ Ruler	(page 6)	
❑ Pattern shears	(page 7)	
❑ Grozing/breaking pliers	(page 7)	
❑ Needle-nose pliers	(page 8)	
❑ Carborundum stone	(page 8)	
❑ Copper foil	(page 9)	One spool
❑ 20-gauge wire	(page 15)	One spool
❑ Wire cutters	(page 8)	
❑ Safety goggles	(page 11)	
❑ Wooden or plastic fid	(page 13)	
❑ Patina	(page 14)	One bottle
❑ Lamp vase cap	(page 94)	One, 3 inches in diameter, with 6 sides
❑ Rubber gloves	(page 14)	
❑ Paper towels/cleaning rag	(page 15)	
❑ Flux remover	(page 14)	
❑ Finishing compound	(page 14)	One bottle
❑ Carbon paper	(page 16)	At least one large sheet
❑ Oak tag	(page 16)	At least one large sheet
❑ Tracing paper	(page 16)	At least one large sheet
❑ Electrical tape	(page 92)	One roll
❑ Plastic basin and sponge	(page 15)	
❑ Thumbtacks and jig material	(page 15)	One complete kit
❑ Rubber cement	(page 16)	One bottle
❑ Colored pencils	(page 16)	
❑ Dustpan and brush	(page 11)	

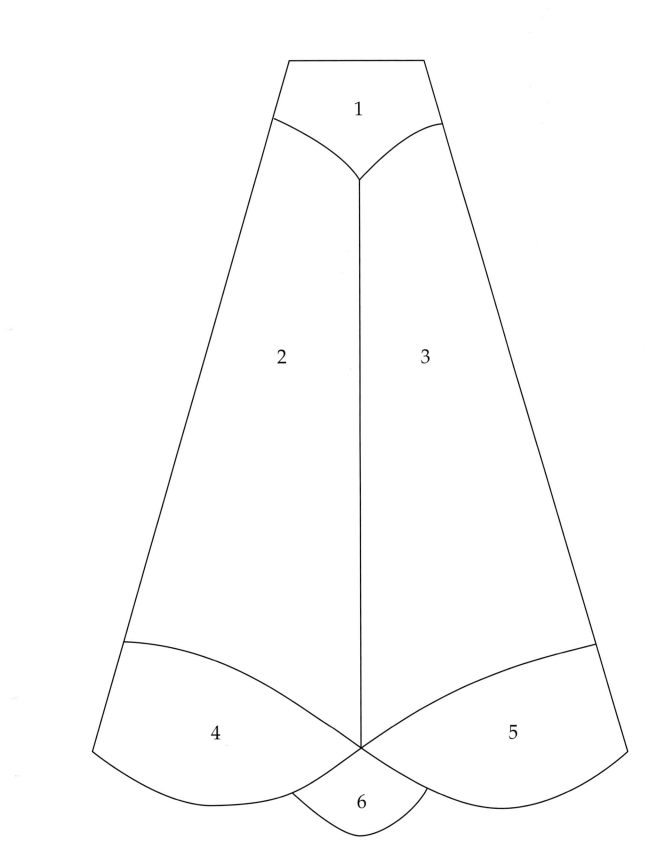

Actual Size

1. Trace the pattern for the lamp panel onto a piece of heavy-stock paper with a ballpoint pen or hard lead pencil, as explained on page 54. Make sure to draw arrows to indicate the direction in which you want the texture of your glass pieces to run so you remember to cut them accordingly.

2. Photocopy the original so that you have six total patterns for the glass panels. You can make the lines on the pattern bolder by drawing over them with a felt-tipped marker.

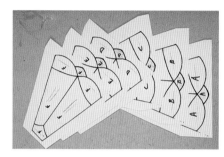

You can also mark the pattern with colored pencils so you don't forget your color choices when selecting glass.

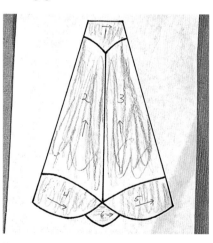

3. Cut out the individual pieces of the pattern, taking care to note the direction you wish the pattern in the glass to follow. Here, the markings indicate that the main pieces will flow up and down, while the smaller pieces will flow from side to side.

4. Make sure your Homasote board or preferred work surface is in place.

5. Use rubber cement to glue the six pieces of the pattern onto the stained glass you have chosen. Arrange them to make the best use of the glass and prevent unnecessary waste.

6. Cut out the shapes, grind the edges of the pieces until they are smooth, and clean them.

7. Wrap each piece in copper foil.

Beginners should work on one panel at a time to avoid confusion and mix-ups with pieces of similar appearance.

8. Frame the pattern with three pieces of metal jig material on the top and on both sides to keep the pieces of the panel together while you work.

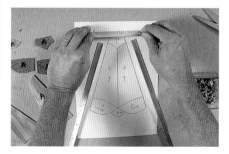

9. Use tacks or pushpins to secure the metal slats.

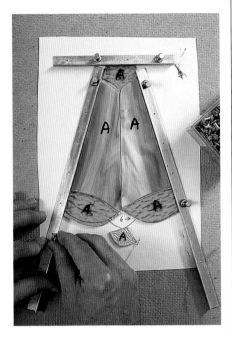

10. Secure the bottom edges of the three smaller pieces of stained glass with tacks or pushpins.

11. Apply flux to joint areas to prime them for tack soldering. Focus on areas where three seams meet, such as near the top and bottom of the panel.

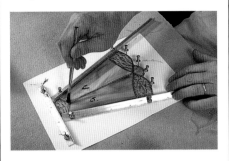

12. Tack solder the areas where the flux was used. Remember, a bead the size of a small pea is all that is needed at this point for each joint.

Remove the glass from the metal support slats for better access while soldering.

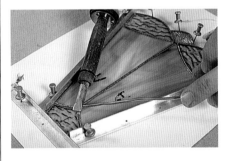

13. Fill in all of the interior seams with an even layer of solder.

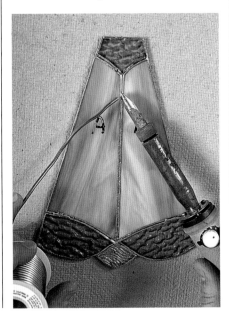

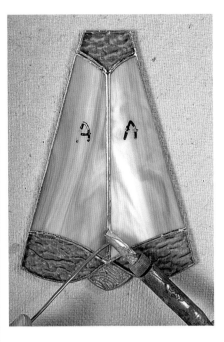

14. Repeat this process on the remaining five panels.

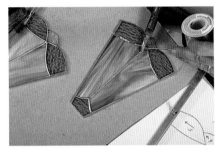

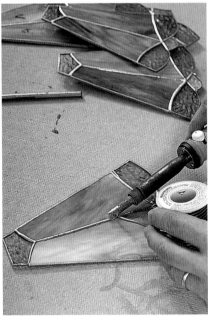

Clean each panel with warm water and detergent.

15. Arrange the six glass panels in a semicircle, with about $^1/_8$ inch separating each panel. Make sure the tops and bottoms of the panels are aligned evenly.

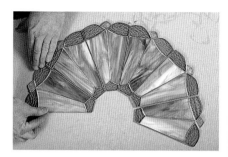

16. Starting with one of the two end panels, place a piece of standard electrical tape over the gap between it and the adjacent panel. Press firmly to make sure the tape sticks. The tape will hold the panels together while acting as a hinge of sorts during later steps in the project.

Repeat this step for the remaining four seams.

17. Apply a semicircle of electrical tape near the top of the panels, as shown. Leave about an inch of excess tape hanging over the edge of the first panel; this flange of tape will be put to use in a few moments. Press firmly on the tape to make sure it sticks.

18. Apply a larger semicircle of electrical tape near the bottom edge, as shown. Again, make sure to leave about an inch of excess tape hanging over the edge.

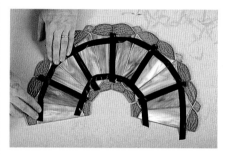

19. Grip the top edges of the six panels simultaneously and pull them upward while bringing the two ends toward each other. The bottom parts of the panels will help steady the project as you raise it up.

20. When the first and last panels touch, press the two flanges of excess tape into place to hold the project together.

21. Apply flux to one of the spots where the two top panels meet.

22. Apply solder to that spot.

23. Check to make sure the top panel pieces are in alignment.

Adjust them if they are not.

24. Hold the panels in place, if necessary, and apply a bead of solder to the joint.

25. Repeat this step for all remaining top joints.

26. Tack solder the joints at the bottom of the glass panels.

27. When all of the joints have been tack soldered into place, the opening at the top of the lampshade will measure 3 inches across.

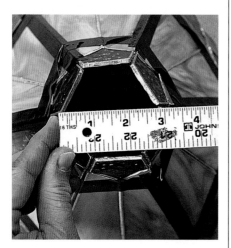

28. Select a lamp vase cap made of brass or other quality material with a diameter of 3 inches. Remove any dirt and corrosion from it with a piece of steel wool.

29. Apply flux on every part of the topside of the vase cap, including the edges that face outward. There is no need to flux the underside of the cap because it will be hidden from view on the finished project.

30. Apply a thin, even layer of solder to completely tin the surface of the cap. Some black areas will likely form as the hot tin and brass react with each other. This is easily removable when cool.

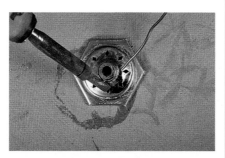

31. Place the handle of the flux brush or other sticklike tool through the center of the cap to hold it at an angle while soldering the bottom edge.

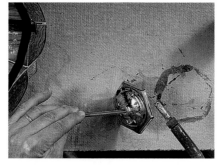

32. Wipe away discolored areas with a towel.

33. Measure and cut a section of 20-gauge wire that will rim the top edge of the lamp for added structural support.

34. Apply flux to the copper edges of the top rim.

35. Apply flux to the wire.

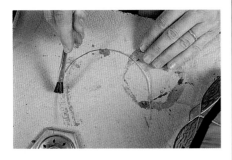

36. Place one end of the wire on the edge of one of the glass panels and tack solder it into place. Then, continue around the rim, bending the wire into place and holding it there until you add a bead of solder to it.

37. Snip the wire where it meets the first solder point.

38. Apply an even layer of solder around the top rim.

39. Place the cap on the top of the shade.

40. Flux the pointed areas on the cap where they touch the foiled seams of the glass panels.

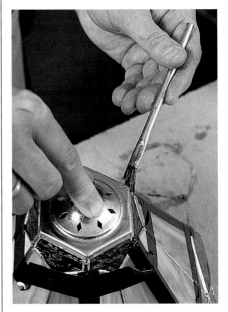

41. Apply solder to these points to attach the cap.

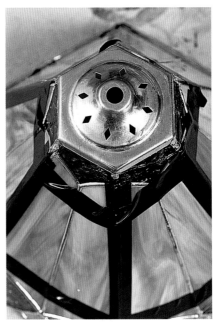

42. Carefully turn the lamp over to gain access to the underside. Flux all of the copper seams there.

43. Apply solder to fill in these seams evenly.

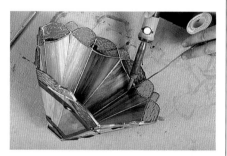

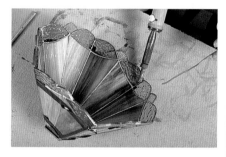

44. Turn the lamp over and remove the pieces of electrical tape. This will reveal the copper seams that have not been soldered up to this point.

45. Apply flux to these seams.

46. At this point, you might find lamp wedges to be helpful for supporting the shade while it is on its side. The wedges are not mandatory; they just add greater stability while applying solder. The wedges consist of a large back piece covered in rubberized foam for gripping power. Two small wedges made of the same material are used in the front; their design makes them sturdy and slip-resistant.

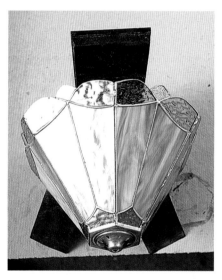

47. Fill in the remaining seams with an even coating of solder.

48. Measure and cut a section of 20-gauge wire to run along the bottom edge of the lamp, giving it added structural support.

49. Apply flux to the copper edges of the bottom rim.

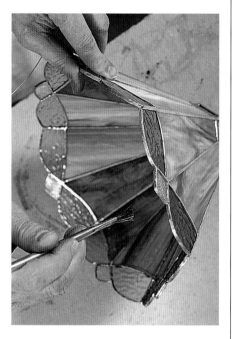

50. Apply flux to the wire.

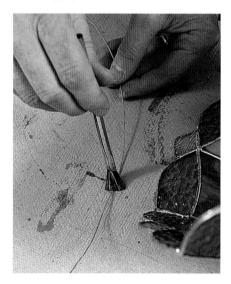

51. Place one end of the wire on the edge of one of the glass panels and tack solder it into place.

52. Continue around the rim, bending the wire into place and holding it there until you add a bead of solder to it.

53. Continue this process until your wire meets with the first spot you soldered; snip the wire.

54. Apply flux to the end of the wire and solder it in place.

55. Apply an even layer of solder over the entire length of wire and then clean the piece.

The silvery solder can be darkened with patina at this point if you choose. Put on a pair of rubber gloves, because patina is caustic and may burn skin. Apply it to the soldered joints with a sponge. When finished, clean the lampshade with warm, soapy water to remove excess patina and any residue of glass or solder. The darkened portions of the solder will not be affected by water.

Finally, apply flux remover to the glass. Your lampshade is now ready to be placed onto a lamp.

9

Holiday Candle

Time investment: 2–3 hours total

There is virtually no limit to the variety of small lead projects that you can make. If something can be symbolically recreated through the use of stained glass pieces, lead cames, and solder, then chances are someone has designed a basic pattern for it. These little projects, sometimes referred to as sun catchers, make perfect gifts because they can be made with a person's interests in mind: flowers, musical instruments, sporting goods, religious items, fruits, animals, insects, celestial bodies, and on and on.

Like most kinds of stained glass projects, the difficulty level can vary from pattern to pattern, typically because of the number of glass pieces involved and the kinds of cuts needed in the glass. Because these projects require few materials, they are good for experimentation and practice, too.

SHOPPING LIST: Holiday Candle

You need less than a quarter of a square foot of glass each for the white, green, and amber pieces. You will also need four red glass nuggets. You might be able to find a stained glass shop that will sell you glass scraps for use in small projects such as this. Keep in mind, though, that many stained glass suppliers won't sell anything smaller than a square foot of glass at one time. Please note that glass estimates factor in some excess material to allow for a few mistakes.

Item		Quantity
❏ Glass cutter	(pages 3–4)	
❏ Cutting oil	(page 4)	One bottle
❏ Soldering iron	(page 5)	
❏ Solder	(page 5)	One spool
❏ Flux	(page 6)	One bottle
❏ Flux brush	(page 6)	
❏ Ruler	(page 6)	
❏ Pattern shears	(page 7)	
❏ Grozing/breaking pliers	(page 7)	
❏ Needle-nose pliers	(page 8)	
❏ Carborundum stone	(page 8)	
❏ Lead came	(page 10)	A strip $3^1/2$ to 4 feet long of $^1/_{16}$-inch U-channel
❏ Lead cutters	(page 11)	
❏ Safety goggles	(page 11)	
❏ Wooden or plastic fid	(page 13)	
❏ Paper towels/cleaning rag	(page 15)	
❏ Flux remover	(page 14)	
❏ Finishing compound	(page 14)	One bottle
❏ Carbon paper	(page 16)	At least one large sheet
❏ Oak tag	(page 16)	At least one large sheet
❏ Tracing paper	(page 16)	At least one large sheet
❏ Plastic basin and sponge	(page 15)	
❏ Rubber cement	(page 16)	One bottle
❏ Colored pencils	(page 16)	
❏ Dustpan and brush	(page 11)	

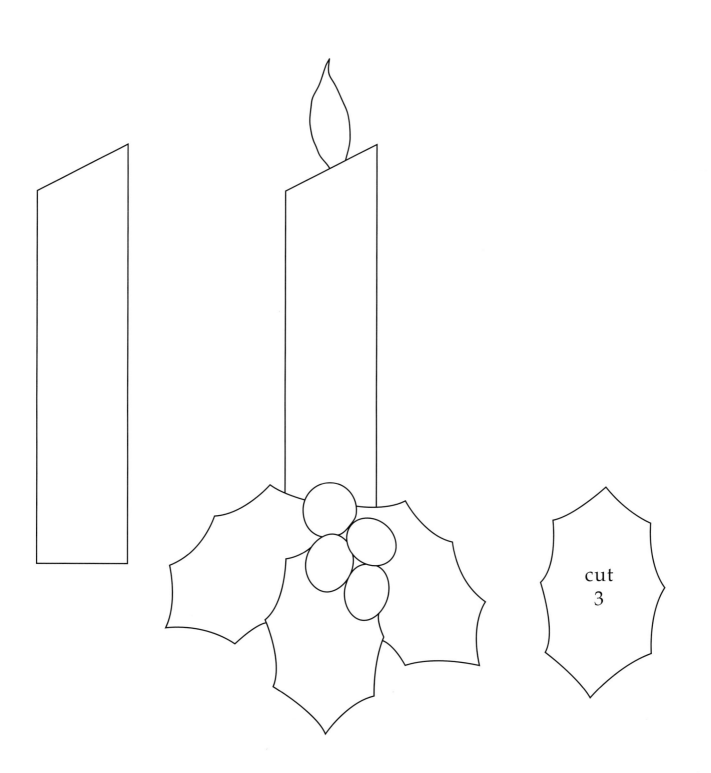

Enlarge 125%

Holiday Candle

1. Copy the pattern for the project.

2. Trace the pattern onto a piece of heavy-stock paper with a ballpoint pen or hard lead pencil. Cut out the shapes for the candle body, the holly leaf, and the candle flame with regular scissors.

You do not need to cut out the circles indicating berries because pre-cut glass nuggets will be used.

3. Trace a single outline of the candle body and flame onto your pieces of glass and use a glass cutter to remove them. Trace three holly leaves on a sheet of glass and cut them out.

The candle will come together with the center holly leaf overlapping the two on either side of it; the candle flame simply sits atop the main part of the candle.

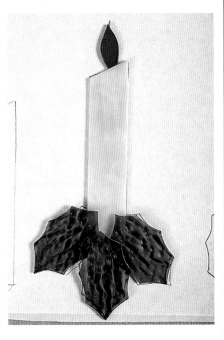

The berries are used mainly on the center leaf and slightly above it to cover the top edges where the leaves meet.

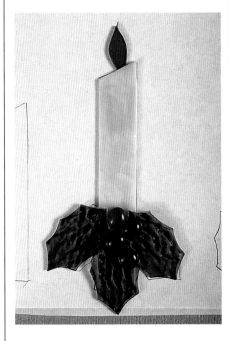

4. Make sure your Homasote board or preferred work surface is in place.

5. Take an 18-inch piece of lead came with a single U-channel and place the bottom edge of the candle piece into it. Begin bending the malleable lead around the perimeter of the candle.

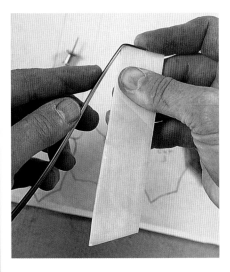

6. Hold the lead firmly in place against the edge of the candle as you continue wrapping the came.

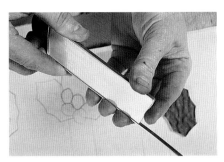

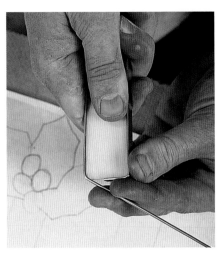

7. Mark the end of the lead came where it meets with the front edge. A tack or nail will work fine to scratch a line on the lead.

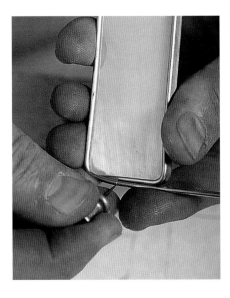

8. Cut the came straight across with lead pliers. Use a quick snipping motion to produce a clean cut.

9. Use a brush to apply flux to the spot where the two ends of the came touch.

10. Heat the soldering iron; apply solder to hold the came together. Like all projects that use lead cames, the glass will sit in the U-shaped channel somewhat loosely. That means that, properly wrapped, the glass might rattle a bit when handled and touched; you should not, however, be able to remove the glass from the lead without effort.

11. Wrap a piece of lead came around the piece of glass that will serve as the candle's flame.

12. Continue wrapping until the lead encircles the glass.

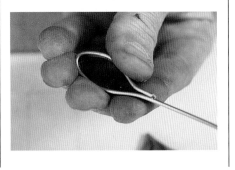

13. Use lead pliers to snip through both the top and bottom sections of lead. Cut at an angle to help preserve the pointed aspect of the candle flame.

14. The cut will expose the gap in the two pieces of lead.

15. Apply flux to this spot, and apply solder to fill in the gap.

16. Wrap each of the three glass leaves in a lead strip. Press the lead firmly onto the edge of glass so that it hugs the contours well.

17. Use lead pliers to snip the top and bottom pieces of the lead cames. Cut at an angle to maintain the pointed look of the leaf.

18. Flux the gap caused by the cutting of the lead and fill it in with solder.

19. Wrap each of the glass berries in lead.

20. Use lead pliers to cut the strip flush where both ends meet. The soft properties of the lead will allow you to cut a section that makes an almost perfect loop.

21. Apply flux to the edges of the lead.

22. Apply a bead of solder to hold the strip together.

23. Use the pattern to align the flame and the candle body.

24. Apply flux to the spot where the two pieces touch.

25. Solder the two pieces together.

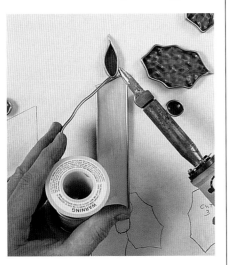

26. Position the left holly leaf on top of the candle body, using the pattern underneath as a rough guide. Apply flux to the two spots where the leaf edge meets the candle edge at the top and bottom edge.

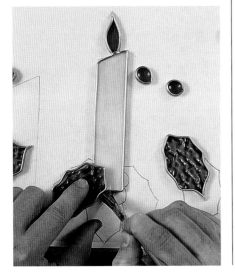

27. Solder the leaf onto the candle at those two points.

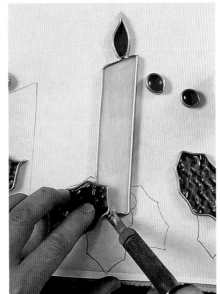

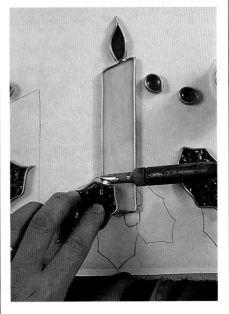

28. Position the right holly leaf, using the paper pattern as a guide, and apply flux the same way you did with the previous piece.

29. Solder it into place as you did with the other leaf.

30. Center the last leaf between the other two, as shown, and apply flux at all of the points where two pieces of lead touch.

31. Apply solder to hold the central leaf in place.

32. Place the four glass berries on the holly leaves and arrange them to your taste.

33. Hold them steady and brush on flux.

34. Apply solder to attach the berries to the leaves and to attach them to each other for added strength.

The project will have a layered look when viewed from the side because of the manner in which the leaves are stacked.

35. Use pliers to hold an O-ring against the lead at the tip of the candle. Apply flux to both the hoop and the lead.

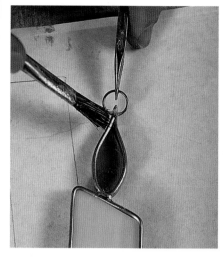

36. Solder the hoop to the candle flame.

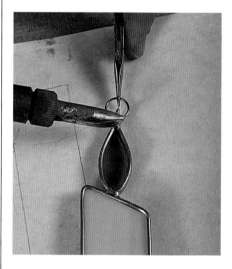

37. The finished project can be hung up in a window the way you would a traditional piece of stained glass, or it can simply be used as a display piece placed on an end table, mantel, or windowsill.

10

Three-Dimensional Hanging Star

Time investment: 2–3 hours total

This three-dimensional star represents a change of pace from the flat-panel projects detailed in the book thus far. You will use the same basic skills of cutting, grinding, and foiling glass pieces that you did in the first several projects. With the hanging star, though, soldering is a little bit trickier because certain pieces are put together perpendicular to each other. A steady hand and a careful eye are perhaps the two most important tools you will need to successfully complete this geometric delight, in which the point of each piece of cut glass faces outward. Appropriate for holiday displays or general decorating all year long, this shimmering star radiates like a true work of art.

This project requires about 1 square foot of glass; the glass shown is a clear iridescent with a texture that makes it resemble thin slabs of ice. Remember, the type, color, and texture of glass chosen to illustrate each of the projects in this book are merely suggestions; let your own creativity and sense of aesthetics be your guide when picking materials.

SHOPPING LIST: Three-Dimensional Hanging Star

This project requires about 1 square foot of glass. Please note that glass estimates factor in some excess material to allow for a few mistakes.

Item		Quantity
❑ Glass cutter	(pages 3–4)	
❑ Cutting oil	(page 4)	One bottle
❑ Soldering iron	(page 5)	
❑ Solder	(page 5)	One spool
❑ Flux	(page 6)	One bottle
❑ Flux brush	(page 6)	
❑ Ruler	(page 6)	
❑ Pattern shears	(page 7)	
❑ Grozing/breaking pliers	(page 7)	
❑ Needle-nose pliers	(page 8)	
❑ Carborundum stone	(page 8)	
❑ Copper foil	(page 9)	One spool
❑ 20-gauge wire	(page 15)	One spool
❑ Wire cutters	(page 8)	
❑ Safety goggles	(page 11)	
❑ Wooden or plastic fid	(page 13)	
❑ Paper towels/cleaning rag	(page 15)	
❑ Flux remover	(page 14)	
❑ Finishing compound	(page 14)	One bottle
❑ Carbon paper	(page 16)	At least one large sheet
❑ Oak tag	(page 16)	At least one large sheet
❑ Tracing paper	(page 16)	At least one large sheet
❑ Plastic basin and sponge	(page 15)	
❑ Thumbtacks and jig material	(page 15)	One complete kit
❑ Rubber cement	(page 16)	One bottle
❑ Colored pencils	(page 16)	
❑ Dustpan and brush	(page 11)	

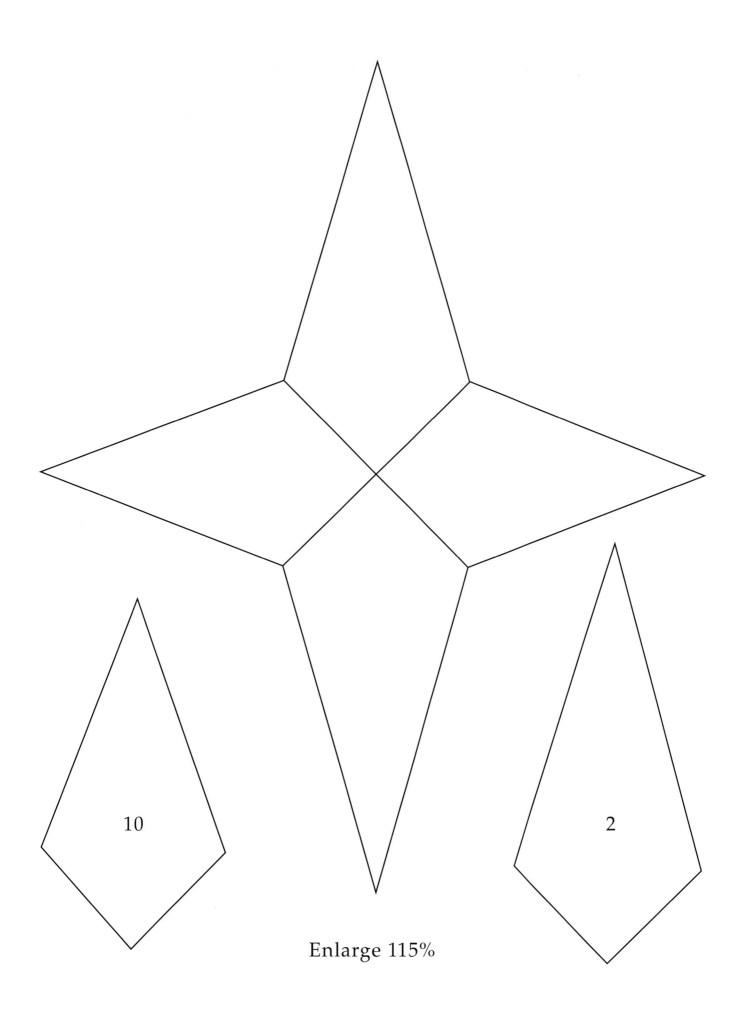

10

2

Enlarge 115%

1. Copy the pattern for the project.

2. Trace the pattern onto a piece of heavy-stock paper with a ballpoint pen or hard lead pencil. Cut out the two geometric shapes at the bottom of the pattern with regular scissors.

3. Trace the outline of the larger geometric shape twice on the glass you have chosen. Trace the smaller shape 10 times onto the glass. Reduce wasted glass by positioning the shapes close together.

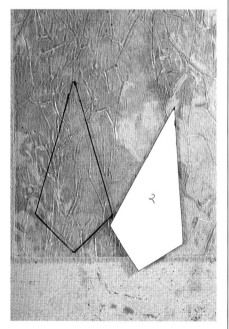

4. Make sure your Homasote board or preferred work surface is in place.

5. Use a glass cutter and ruler or other straight-edge tool to cut out all of the shapes.

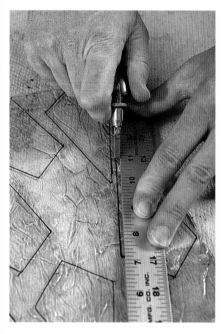

6. Grind the edges of each piece until smooth and then clean them. See page 44 for tips about grinding by hand or with a machine.

7. Apply foil to edges of each piece and set them aside.

8. The basic frame of the ornament is made up of the two larger pieces on the top and bottom of the pattern as shown, and two of the smaller pieces on the left and right.

9. The copper foil around the edges of each piece of glass must first be tinned—coated with a thin layer of solder—before the project can be assembled. First, use a brush to apply flux along the edges of each of the 12 pieces.

10. Heat the soldering iron and apply a few drops of solder to the foil. Use the tip of the iron to spread the solder evenly, adding more solder as needed.

11. Turn the piece at an angle to allow the solder to flow downward along outside edges. Repeat this process on the remaining 11 shapes.

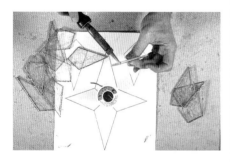

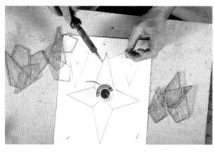

12. Place the two larger pieces and two of the smaller pieces on top of the pattern.

13. Use pushpins to hold the four pieces of the star in place.

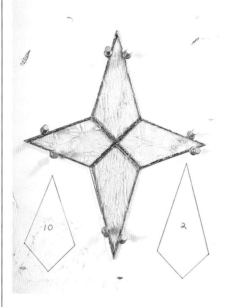

14. Solder the pieces together along the inside edges that form an X. Make sure the solder is smooth and not lumpy.

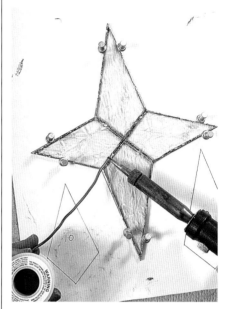

15. Let the piece cool for about 30 seconds. This will be the structure that holds the remainder of the pieces.

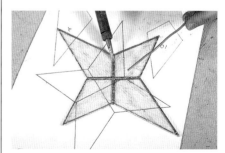

16. Place the edge of a piece of glass along the soldered middle seam at a right angle, with the sharp point facing outward as shown. When joined with solder, the pieces will have a bit of suppleness along the seam to correct errors, but you can save yourself some effort with good placement before each solder.

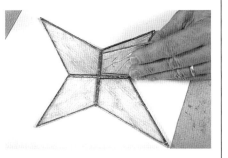

17. Hold the piece firmly in position with one hand and apply solder along both sides of the bottom edge with the other. The cooled solder will hold the piece in place.

18. Align another piece of glass as shown and apply solder.

19. At this point, you can make slight adjustments to make sure the pieces are straight.

20. Hold a piece of glass along the soldered seam at a right angle.

Solder it into place.

21. Align another piece of glass as shown and apply solder. Let the solder cool for about 30 seconds.

22. Gently move the pieces until they line up to form an X.

23. Apply solder to the center of the pieces to hold them all together.

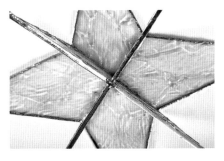

24. Tip the project up on end, with one of the larger points sticking up as shown. Apply solder to the copper foil on the inside edges of each piece, turning the star as you go.

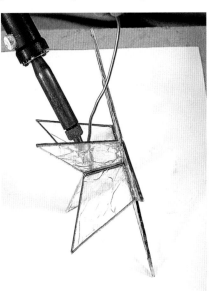

25. Place the project flat on your work surface, using the bottom four star points as "legs" to support it.

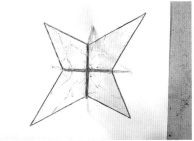

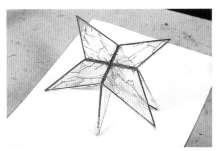

26. Fill in the center seams with an even layer of solder.

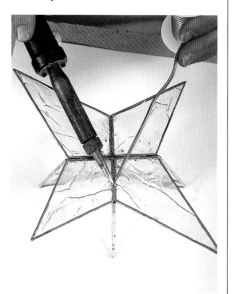

27. Hold a piece of glass perpendicular to the main project, as shown, and solder into place.

28. Align another piece of glass and solder it into place.

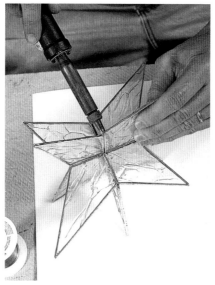

29. Place a piece of glass at a right angle and solder it into place.

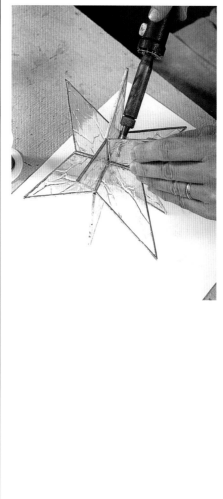

30. Repeat the process with another piece on the other side, as shown.

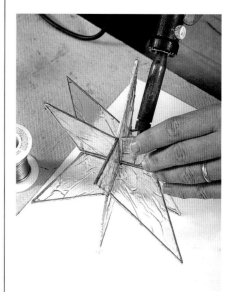

31. Make sure the four pieces you just soldered form an X, and then solder the central point where they meet to hold them together.

32. Solder all inside seams of these pieces, turning the project as needed for access. Examine the ornament carefully. There are a number of seams that need to be soldered, and some tend to play hide and seek with you!

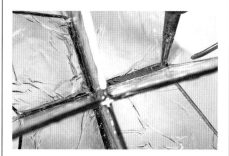

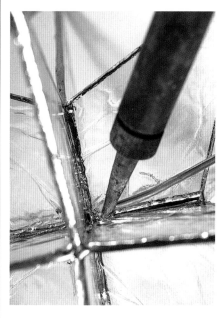

33. Cut a strand of 20-gauge copper wire for use as a hanger.

34. Even out the tips of the wire and twist them several times to form a loop.

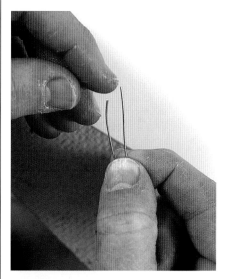

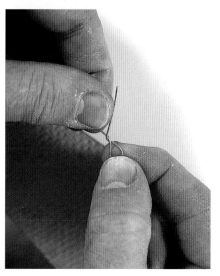

35. Apply flux to the wire.

TIP

Use thin wire, such as the type sold at picture framing or craft stores, or strong fishing line to hang the ornament.

36. Place the wire over the tip of one of the large star shapes and solder into place.

The finished loop attachment will look like this:

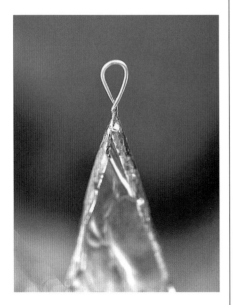

37. As a final step, spray the ornament with flux remover and wipe it dry.

11

Mirror with Flower Overlay

Time investment: 2–3 hours total

This project introduces you to working with mirrored glass, which is different from other types of glass only in that a reflective coating has been added to the backside of it. Mirrored glass sold at stained glass or craft shops cuts the same way as regular stained glass. Special care must be taken to avoid damaging the reflective coating; in fact, you will be instructed about how to apply a spray coating of sealer to protect the mirror.

With this project, the main mirrored piece is made up of a series of glass pieces soldered together around a central oval of mirrored glass; on top of this main piece is a detailed flower attached by solder at numerous spots. The effect is quite charming. Completing the project requires the same basic skills of cutting, grinding, and foiling glass pieces that you learned by completing earlier projects in this book.

117

SHOPPING LIST: Mirror with Flower Overlay

You will need about 1 square foot of stained glass for the pieces that make up the flower, plus 1 square foot of mirrored glass. Please note that glass estimates factor in some excess material to allow for a few mistakes.

Item		Quantity
❏ Glass cutter	(pages 3–4)	
❏ Cutting oil	(page 4)	One bottle
❏ Soldering iron	(page 5)	
❏ Solder	(page 5)	One spool
❏ Flux	(page 6)	One bottle
❏ Flux brush	(page 6)	
❏ Ruler	(page 6)	
❏ Pattern shears	(page 7)	
❏ Grozing/breaking pliers	(page 7)	
❏ Needle-nose pliers	(page 8)	
❏ Carborundum stone	(page 8)	
❏ Copper foil	(page 9)	One spool
❏ Lead came	(page 10)	A 3-foot strip of $1/4$-inch U-channel
❏ Lead cutter	(page 11)	
❏ Horseshoe nails	(page 11)	About a dozen
❏ Safety goggles	(page 11)	
❏ Wooden or plastic fid	(page 13)	
❏ Patina	(page 14)	One bottle
❏ Rubber gloves	(page 14)	
❏ Paper towels/cleaning rag	(page 15)	
❏ Flux remover	(page 14)	
❏ Finishing compound	(page 14)	One bottle
❏ Mirror sealer	(page 14)	
❏ Carbon paper	(page 16)	At least one large sheet
❏ Oak tag	(page 16)	At least one large sheet
❏ Tracing paper	(page 16)	At least one large sheet
❏ Plastic basin and sponge	(page 15)	
❏ Thumbtacks and jig material	(page 15)	One complete kit
❏ Rubber cement	(page 16)	One bottle
❏ Colored pencils	(page 16)	
❏ Dustpan and brush	(page 11)	

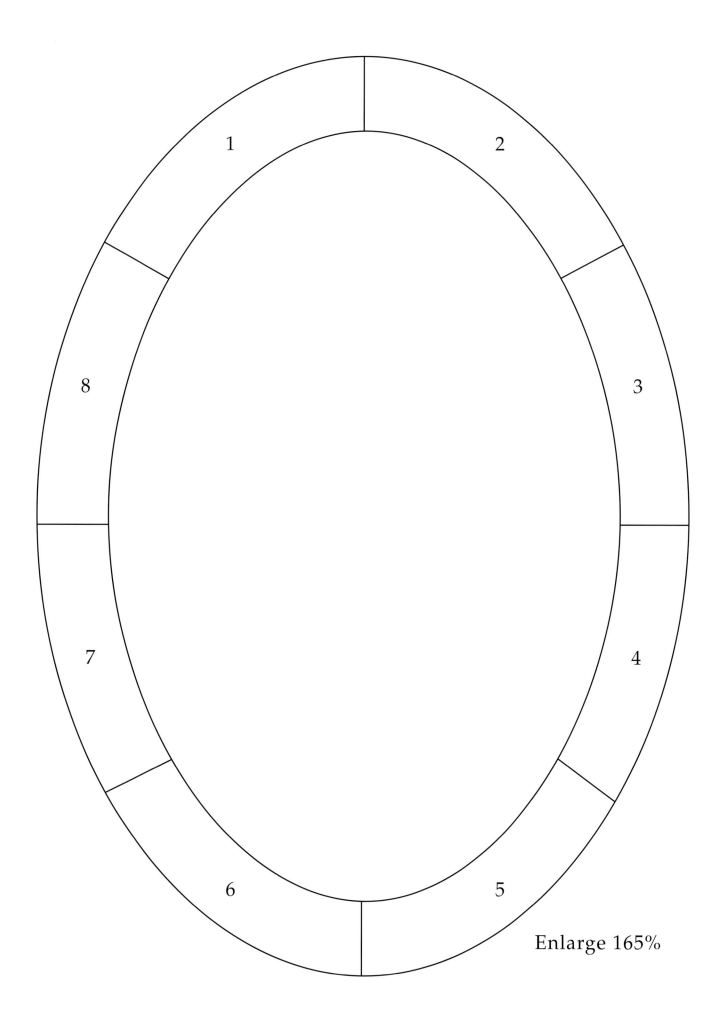

Enlarge 165%

Enlarge 115%

1. Trace the patterns onto a piece of heavy-stock paper with a ballpoint pen or hard lead pencil.

2. Cut out all of the shapes with scissors and use rubber cement to glue them onto the pieces of glass you have selected.

3. Make sure your Homasote board or preferred work surface is in place.

4. Use a glass cutter to cut out all of the shapes. The mirrored glass has cutting properties much the same as stained glass.

5. Grind the edges of each piece until smooth, paying special attention to the edge of the mirror. Make sure you grind any blemished parts where the mirrored backing is marred. Clean the pieces.

6. Put newspapers down on your work surface.

7. Spray the back and edges of the mirrored piece with mirror sealant and then clean it. This will help protect the backing from deteriorating.

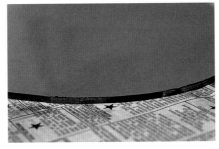

8. Apply copper foil to the edges of all the cut pieces of glass, including the large oval mirror.

9. Place the paper patterns on your work surface and put the pieces together.

10. Use tacks or pushpins to hold all of the pieces together.

11. Tack solder the pieces of the flower so they stay together, then remove the tacks and apply solder to all of the seams more thoroughly. Set this piece aside when finished.

12. Solder the edge pieces so they are attached to the mirror.

13. When you are finished soldering, place a U-shaped piece of lead came around the border of the mirror.

14. Hammer horseshoe nails along the edge to hold it in place.

15. Cut the came at the spot where it meets up with the front edge.

16. Solder this piece together.

17. Turn the piece over and apply flux and solder to the joints on the reverse side.

18. Make a wire hanger for the back of the mirror. Begin by twisting two 4-inch pieces of 20-gauge wire into loops.

19. Apply flux and solder these pieces onto the back of the mirror in the 11 o'clock and 1 o'clock positions.

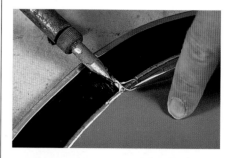

20. Thread a strand of picture hanging wire through one of the loops.

21. Make a knot.

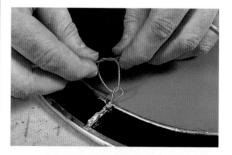

22. Wrap the excess wire around the main strand.

23. Thread the other end of the main strand through the other loop, and make a knot.

24. Pull the knot tight. Use wire cutters to snip to the picture hanging wire.

25. Wrap the excess wire around the main strand.

26. The wire should look like this:

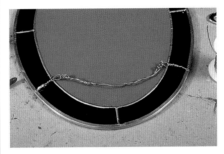

27. Turn the project over and place the flower on top of the mirror. Apply flux to the points where soldered edges of the flower meet soldered points on the mirror.

28. Apply solder to hold the flower firmly in place.

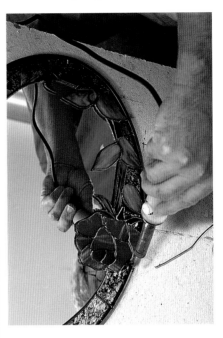

29. Use soap and warm water to clean debris and residue from the project, and then use flux remover and finishing compound to make it shine.

12

Basic Stained Glass Repair

If you make enough stained glass projects, there inevitably will come a time when one of your creations falls on hard times—or actually, a time when something hard falls on one of your creations.

It is disheartening to see one of your projects sustain damage, but there is usually no need to trash the entire piece—especially when only one or two pieces of glass are cracked. A beginner can effect minor stained glass repairs such as the one detailed here. Keep in mind that some repairs should not be tackled by amateurs; heavily damaged pieces should be handled by an expert.

Replacing Broken Glass

1. The best way to begin repairing a piece of stained glass with a single broken panel is to score it repeatedly with a glass cutter, making sure to run the cutting wheel edge to edge in a cross-hatch pattern.

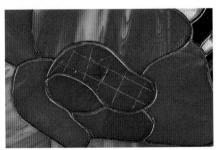

2. Use the ball of the cutter or some other breaking tool to gently tap out loose pieces. Be careful not to strike with too much force. Pieces along the edge may be firmly held by the solder, and impact could break adjoining pieces.

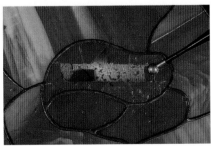

3. Take a piece of steel wool and rub it along the soldered seam of the broken piece to remove oxidized material from it.

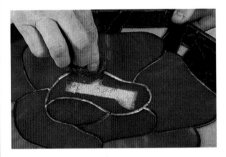

4. Apply flux to the seam.

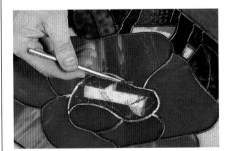

5. Heat your soldering iron. Use the iron to melt the old solder, while at the same time gripping and gently pulling at the broken pieces of glass with pair of pliers or tweezers. It will take a moment or two for the solder to melt away enough to allow you to pull the glass free.

6. Continue to remove the glass in this manner.

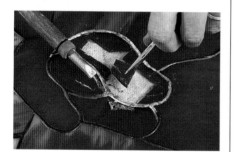

7. When the glass has been removed, the solder will look like this. It is possible at this point to pull the foil off in long strips. Be careful not to grab any of the foiled edges surrounding the good pieces of glass.

8. Use the soldering iron to melt away any remaining solder.

9. Place a piece of plain paper under the missing section and carefully trace the outline.

10. Cut out the shape with scissors.

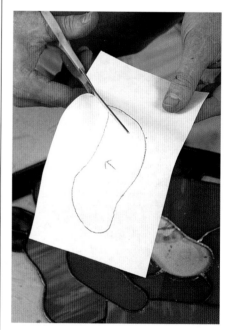

11. Glue the paper to your replacement piece of stained glass. Be sure the glass you select fits well into the color scheme of the existing project. Cut the glass.

12. Grind the shape carefully.

13. Place it in the opening to make sure it fits properly.

14. Apply foil to the edges of the piece.

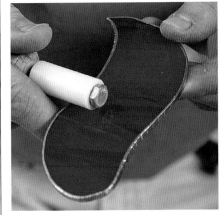

15. Apply flux to the foil.

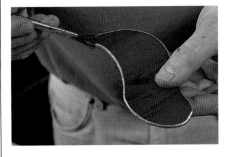

16. Place the glass into the opening and apply solder evenly along the seam.

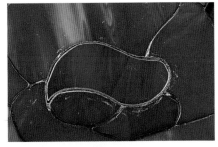

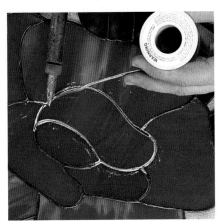

17. Wash away any glass or flux residue.

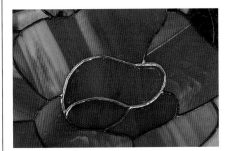

18. Finish the project by applying a little patina to the repaired area, if necessary, for uniformity in the project.

13
Additional Project Patterns

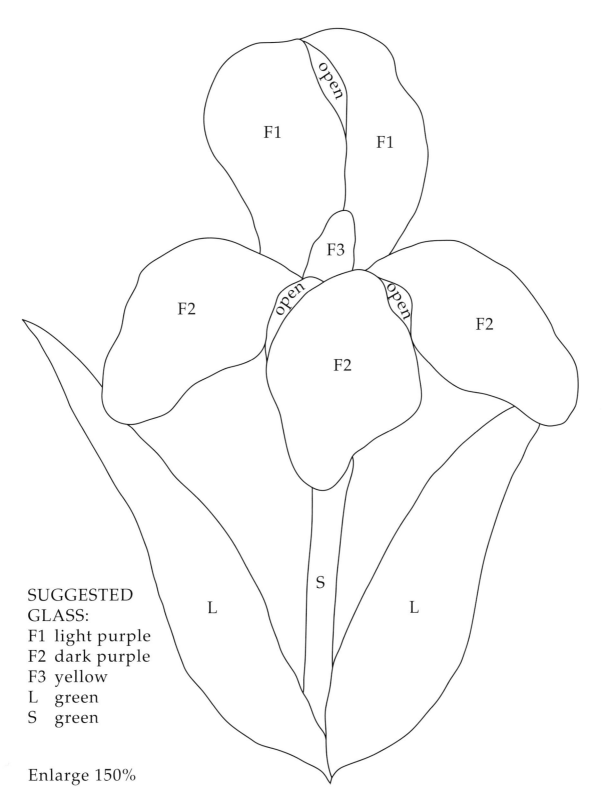

SUGGESTED
GLASS:
F1 light purple
F2 dark purple
F3 yellow
L   green
S   green

Enlarge 150%

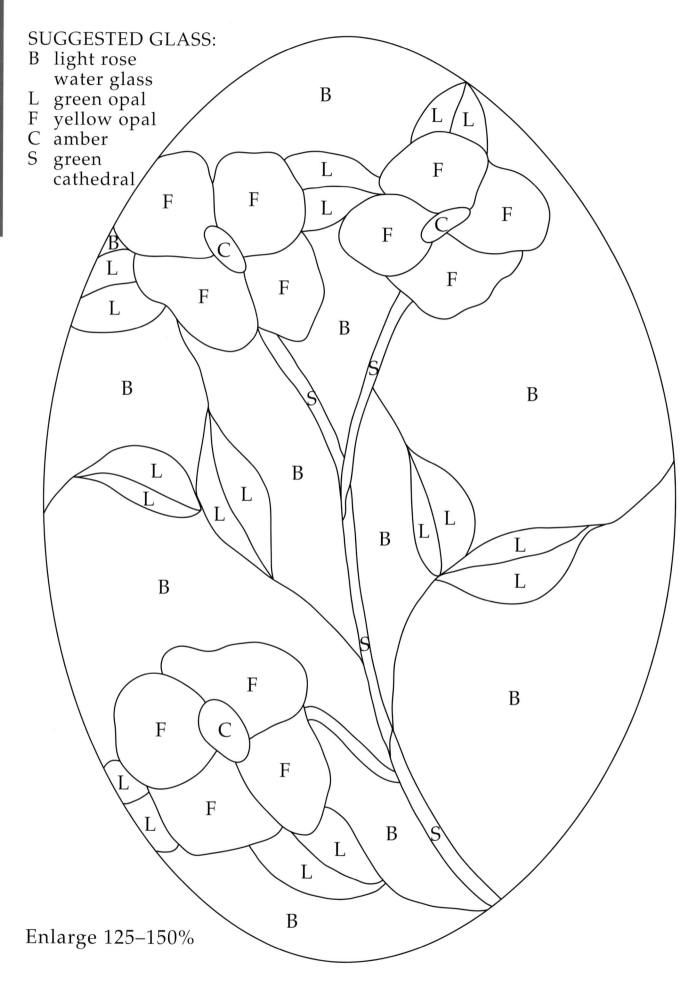

SUGGESTED GLASS:
B light rose
   water glass
L green opal
F yellow opal
C amber
S green
   cathedral

Enlarge 125–150%

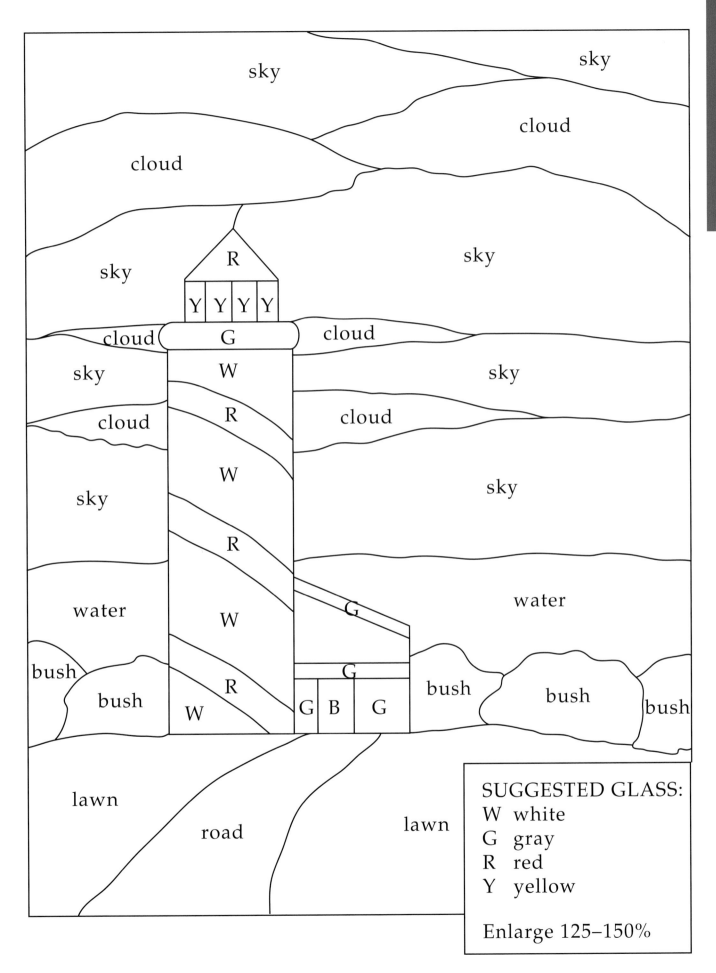

SUGGESTED GLASS:
W   white
G   gray
R   red
Y   yellow

Enlarge 125–150%

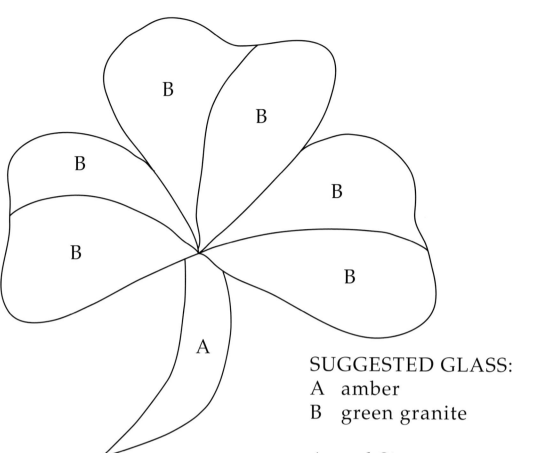

SUGGESTED GLASS:
A   amber
B   green granite

Actual Size

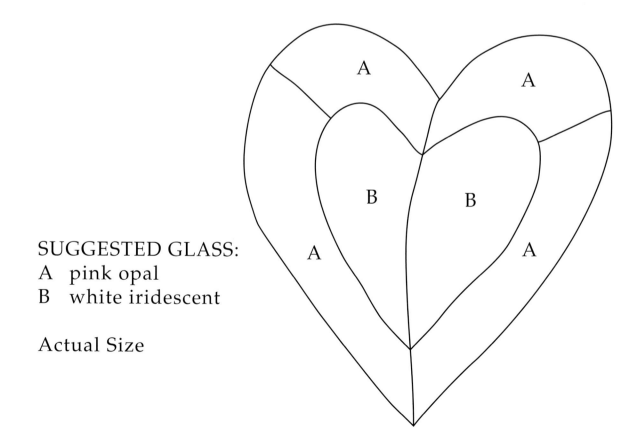

SUGGESTED GLASS:
A   pink opal
B   white iridescent

Actual Size

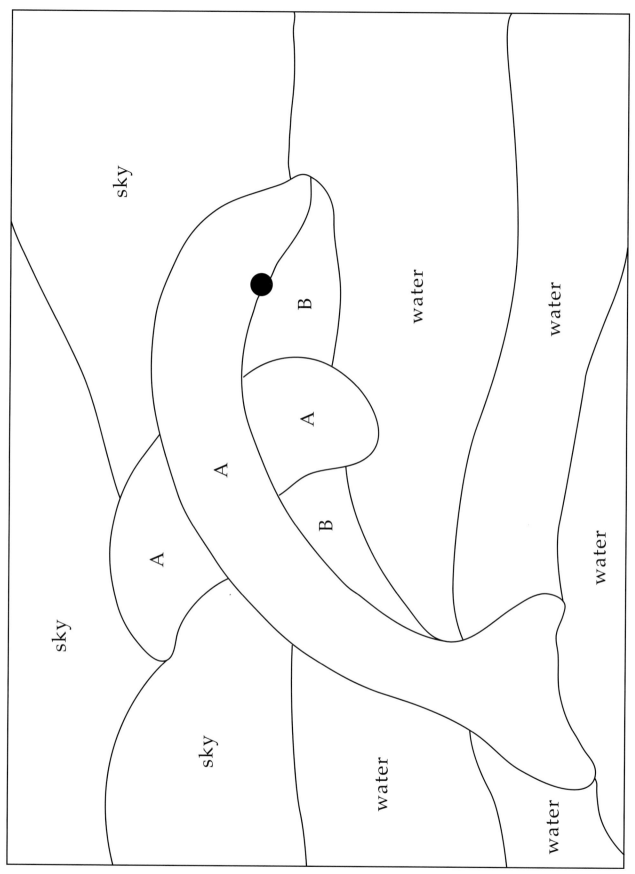

SUGGESTED GLASS:

sky	light blue	A	dark gray
water	dark blue	B	light gray

Enlarge 125–150%

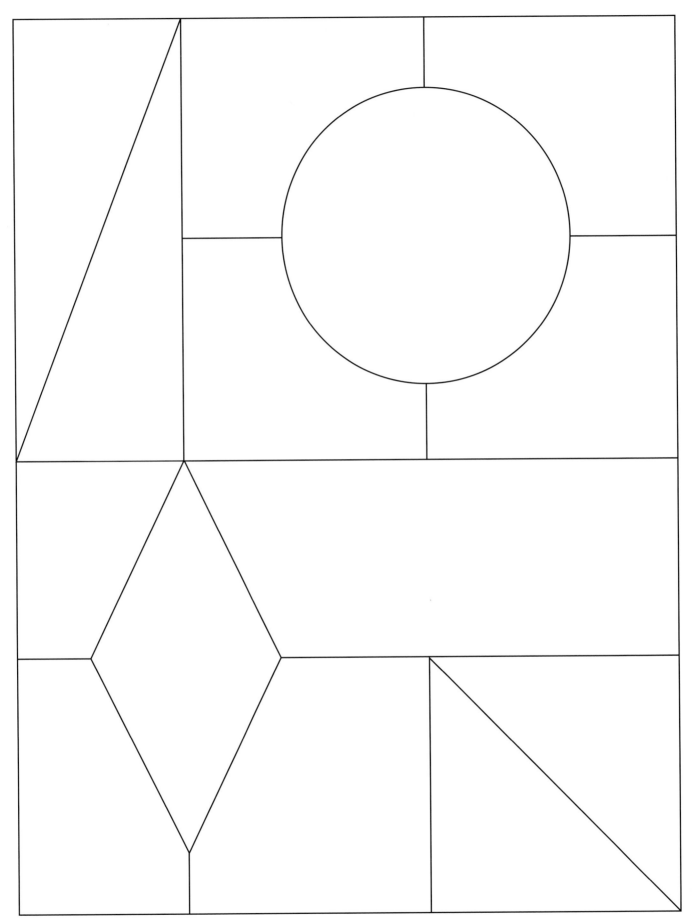

SUGGESTED GLASS AND ENLARGEMENT: At your discretion

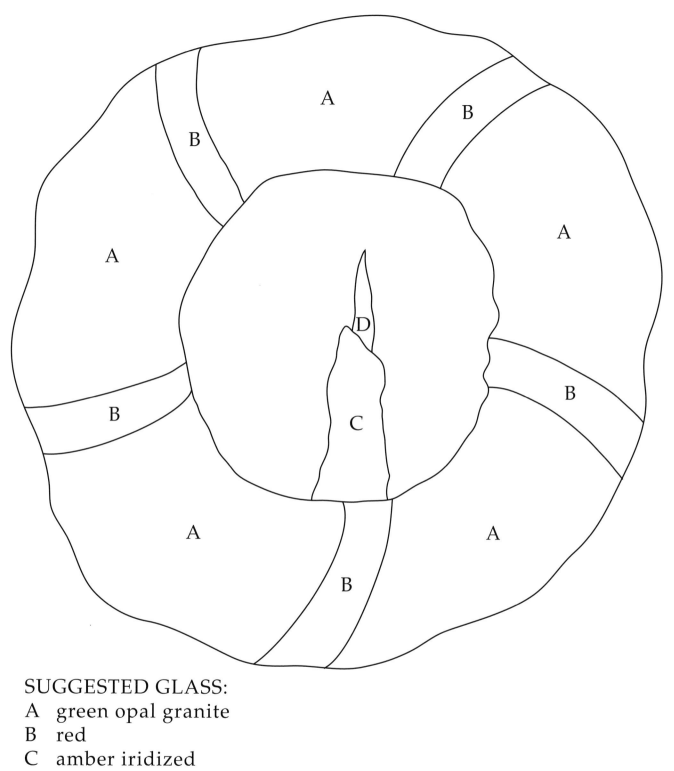

SUGGESTED GLASS:
A   green opal granite
B   red
C   amber iridized
D   yellow

Enlarge 125–150%

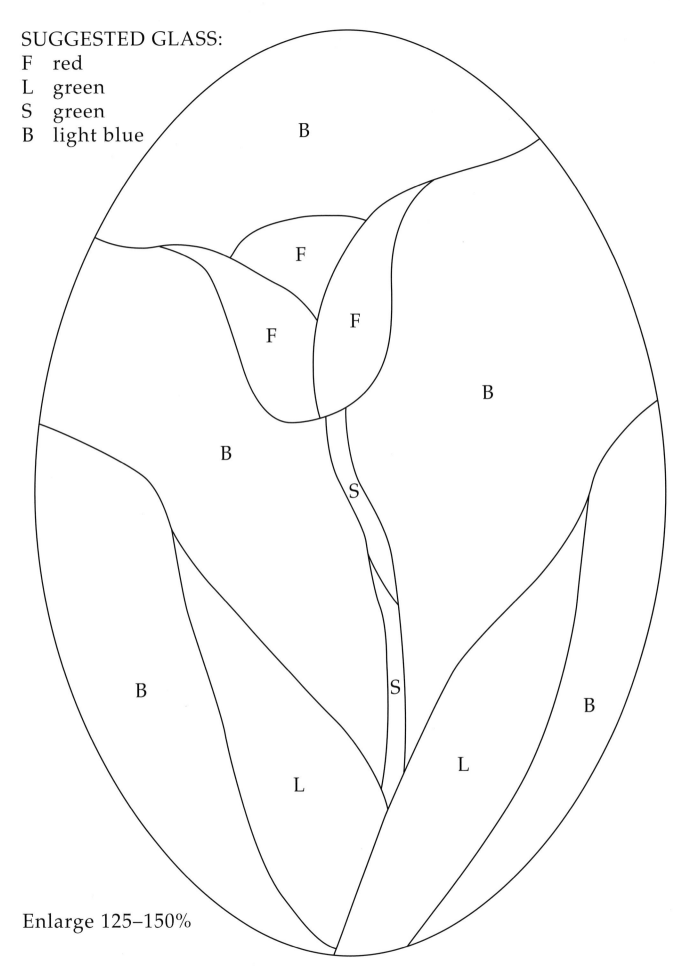

SUGGESTED GLASS:
F   red
L   green
S   green
B   light blue

Enlarge 125–150%

Resources

BOOKS ABOUT STAINED GLASS MAKING

The following titles contain information, projects, and ideas useful to beginners looking to advance their skills.

Bier, Barry. *The Art of Stained Glass Made Easy.* London: New Holland, 1999.

Larson, Alicia. *Stained Glass Secrets.* Aspen, CO: Crystal Images, 1996.

Rich, Chris, with Martha Mitchell and Rachel Ward. *Stained Glass Basics.* New York: Sterling Publishing, 1996.

Wrigley, Lynette. *Stained Glass: Stylish Designs and Practical Projects to Make in a Weekend.* New York: Sterling Publishing, 1999.

RESOURCES ON THE INTERNET

www.rainbowvisionsg.com
Web site of Rainbow Visions Stained Glass in Harrisburg, Pa., owned by expert and consultant Michael Johnston. Contains nice information about all things stained glass, and equipment and materials can be purchased from the company. Numerous stained glass workshops are held regularly, as well.

www.artglassassociation.com
Web site of the Art Glass Association, an international nonprofit group dedicated to the art of stained glass making.

www.inlandcraft.com
Web site of the Inland Craft Products Company, which carries glass grinders and some other equipment used in stained glass making. Also includes a handy state-by-state locator of stained glass retailers.

www.mortonglass.com
Web site of the company that manufactures the Morton system for stained glass cutting. Site also includes plenty of other information about the craft.

www.spectrumglass.com
Web site for the Spectrum Glass Company, a Washington-based manufacturer of specialty sheet glass for use in hobby-craft, fine arts, architecture, lighting, and other applications. Site includes free stained glass patterns that can be downloaded, as well as listings for retailers who sell Spectrum glass.

www.stainedglass.org
Web site of the Stained Glass Association of America. Features an incredible amount of information about the craft, such as its history, profiles of artisans, and details about techniques. Also included is material about lead safety issues as they pertain to stained glass making.

www.stainedglassretailers.com
Web site of Retailers of Art Glass and Supplies (RAGS), a nonprofit organization of owners of retail stores selling stained glass supplies around the world. Includes good information about the craft, as well as listings of nearest suppliers.